BASKETS

New Quilts from an Old Favorite

EDITED BY LINDA BAXTER LASCO

American Quilter's Society
P. O. Box 3290 • Paducah, KY 42002-3290
www.AmericanQuilter.com

Basket Case, detail. Full quilt on page 16.

Thank You Sponsors

JANOME

moda

Located in Paducah, Kentucky, the American Quilter's Society (AQS) is dedicated to promoting the accomplishments of today's quilters. Through its publications and events, AQS strives to honor today's quiltmakers and their work and to inspire future creativity and innovation in quiltmaking.

Executive Book Editor: Andi Milam Reynolds
Senior Editor: Linda Baxter Lasco
Copy Editor: Chrystal Abhalter
Graphic Design: Lynda Smith
Cover Design: Michael Buckingham
Quilt Photography: Charles R. Lynch
Museum Photography: Susan Edwards

©2012, American Quilter's Society

Library of Congress Cataloging-in-Publication Data

Baskets : new quilts from an old favorite / edited by Linda Baxter Lasco.
     pages cm
   Summary: "From the National Quilt Museum's annual New Quilts from an Old Favorite contest, the traditional Basket block is given a new interpretation by the contest winners and finalists"--Provided by publisher.
   ISBN 978-1-60460-019-3
   1. Patchwork--Patterns. 2. Quilting--Patterns. 3. Baskets in art. 4. Quilting--Competitions--United States. I. Lasco, Linda Baxter.
   TT835.B278 2012
   746.46'041--dc23

                              2012002960

Proudly printed and bound in the
United States of America

Attention Photocopying Service: Please note the following—publisher and author give permission to photocopy page 86 for personal use only.

Additional copies of this book may be ordered from the American Quilter's Society, PO Box 3290, Paducah, KY 42002-3290, or online at www.AmericanQuilter.com.

Cover Quilt: First-place winner, Book Plate I, made by Karen Grover, Rockford, Illinois

Title Page: Fibonacci Nebula, made by Patricia Hobbs, Macomb, Illinois

Dedication

This book is dedicated to all those who see a traditional quilt as both a link to the past and a bridge to the future.

"Honoring Today's Quilter"

THE NATIONAL QUILT MUSEUM

The National Quilt Museum is an exciting place where the public can learn about quilts, quiltmaking, quiltmakers, and experience quilts that inspire and delight.

The Museum celebrates the exquisite art of quilting through gallery exhibitions and educational programs. Through its work, the Museum encourages, inspires, and enhances the development of today's quilters.

Contents

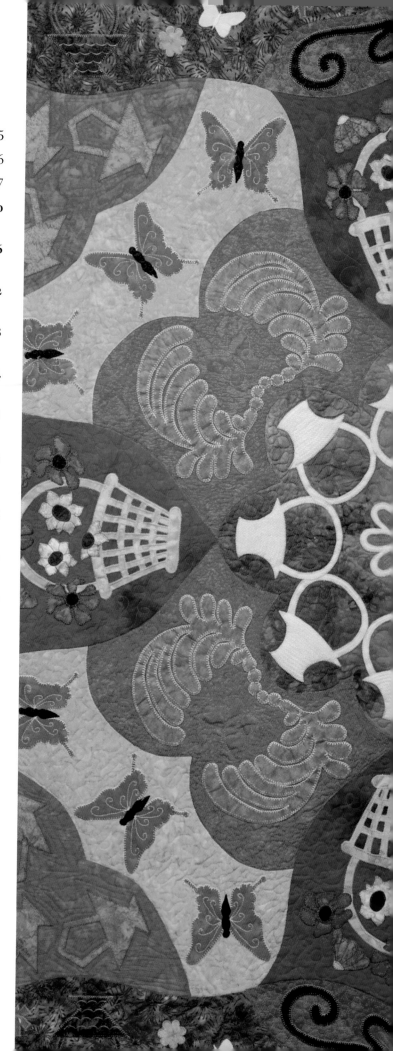

Preface

While preservation of the past is one of a museum's primary functions, its greatest service is performed as it links the past to the present and to the future. With that goal in mind, The National Quilt Museum sponsors an annual contest and exhibit—New Quilts from an Old Favorite (NQOF).

Created both to acknowledge our quiltmaking heritage and to recognize innovation, creativity, and excellence, the contest challenges today's quiltmakers to interpret a single traditional quilt block in a new and exciting work of their own design. Each year contestants respond with a myriad of stunning interpretations.

Baskets: New Quilts from an Old Favorite is a collection of these interpretations. You'll find a brief description of the 2012 contest, followed by the five award winners and fourteen additional finalists and their quilts.

Full-color photographs of the quilts accompany each quiltmaker's comments—comments that provide insight into their widely diverse creative processes. The winners' and finalists' tips, techniques, and patterns offer an artistic framework for your own interpretation. A list of resources and information about The National Quilt Museum are included.

Our wish is that *Baskets: New Quilts from an Old Favorite* will further our quiltmaking heritage as new quilts based on the Basket block are inspired by the outstanding quilts contained within.

Left and opposite: BASKETS, BUTTERFLIES, AND BLOSSOMS, detail.
Full quilt on page 76.

The Contest

Quilts entered in the New Quilts from an Old Favorite contest must be recognizable in some way as a variation of the selected traditional block. The quilts must be no larger than 80" and no smaller than 50" on a side. Each quilt must be quilted. Quilts may only be entered by the maker(s) and must have been completed after December 31 two years prior to the entry date.

Quiltmakers are asked to send in two images—one of the full quilt and one detail shot—for jurying. Three jurors view these images and consider technique, artistry, and interpretation of the theme block to select 18 finalist quilts from among all the entries. These quilts are then sent to the museum where a panel of three judges carefully evaluates them. The evaluation of the actual quilts focuses on design, innovation, theme, and workmanship. The first- through fifth-place winners are selected and the entrants notified.

An exhibit of all the winning and finalist quilts opens at The National Quilt Museum in Paducah, Kentucky, each spring, then travels to venues around the country for two years. Thousands of quilt enthusiasts have enjoyed these exhibits nationwide.

A book is produced by the American Quilter's Society featuring full-color photos of all the quilts, biographical information about each quilter, and tips, techniques, and patterns used in making the quilts. The book provides an inside look at how quilts are created and a glimpse into the artistic mindset of today's quiltmakers.

Previous theme blocks have been Double Wedding Ring, Log Cabin, Ohio Star, Mariner's Compass, Pineapple, Kaleidoscope, Storm at Sea, Bear's Paw, Tumbling Blocks, Feathered Star, Monkey Wrench, Seven Sisters, Dresden Plate, Rose of Sharon, Sawtooth, Burgoyne Surrounded, Sunflower, and Orange Peel. The Jacob's Ladder block has been selected for the 2013 contest and Carolina Lily for 2014.

NQM would like to thank this year's sponsors for their continuing support of this contest: Janome America, Inc., and Moda Fabrics.

Above: BASKET WEAVE, detail. Full quilt on page 42.

Basket Quilts

Basket quilts are particularly appealing, which is reason enough for the choice of the Basket block for this year's New Quilts from an Old Favorite contest. Who doesn't respond positively to a basket of bright flowers or ripe fruit? These symbols of abundance and growth are especially meaningful to all of us. Basket quilts reflect that importance and, if bed-sized, provide warmth as well.

Basket quilts have been made since the early 1800s, but their popularity began in the last quarter of that century. Analysis of the Basket quilts on the Quilt Index (www.quiltindex.org) found 191 Basket quilts that were made between 1840 and 1944. This is also the period when pieced block quilts in general became the dominant quilt form, so it is not surprising that Basket quilts grew in popularity.

The pieced Basket pattern was fairly simple: half-square triangles made up the bowl of the basket and an arced handle was typically appliquéd in place. Flowers may or may not have been added, and they were typically appliquéd, a simple five-lobe blossom.

Fast forward to the 1930s and 1940s. Thirty-two percent of the Quilt Index Basket quilts were made during this period. Appliqué quilts gained popularity with designers and were marketed by Nancy Cabot, Ladies Art Company, *Kansas City Star*, Aunt Martha, and others. Barbara Brackman's *Encyclopedia of Appliqué* lists 11 appliquéd Basket patterns attributed to Nancy Cabot.

Brackman writes that Nancy Cabot was actually Loretta Leitner Rising, who began writing a quilt column for the *Chicago Tribune* in 1933. The name Cabot would have played into the Colonial Revival movement that began after the Civil War and was still going strong in the 1930s. Baskets of flowers were a popular Colonial Revival motif and were frequently seen in medallion quilts of the period. These appliquéd baskets often depicted openwork baskets with outward swooping curved rims, a very romantic counterpoint to the earlier pieced Basket patterns. The *Encyclopedia of Appliqué* lists 46 appliqué designs with the word "Basket" in the title. Of those 46 patterns, 32 are from the 1920s and 1930s. This reinforces the concept of Basket quilts as a Colonial Revival article, and denotes the period of Basket quilts' greatest popularity.

Some of the most striking Basket quilts have been made by the Amish. With brilliant blue and other color pieced baskets glowing on a black or other dark background, these "plain" quilts have a vibrancy not often found in other Basket quilts.

Quilters today enjoy making Basket quilts, particularly in autumn colors. Excellent Basket quilts have been entered in recent American Quilter's Society shows, evidence of continuing popularity of these patterns. The abundance depicted in these quilts endear them to today's audience just as in the past.

Judy Schwender
Curator of Collections/Registrar
The National Quilt Museum

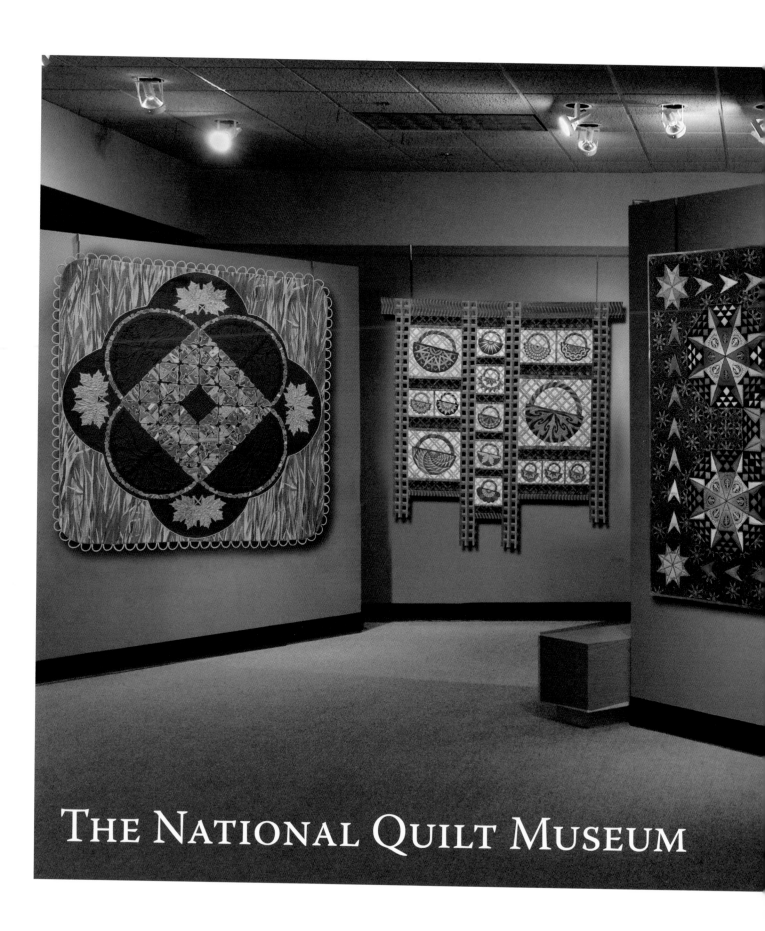

THE NATIONAL QUILT MUSEUM

Photo by Phil Grover

Karen Grover
Rockford, Illinois

Butcher, baker, candlestick maker. For me, it was art student, mother, mechanical engineer, and (not to be forgotten) quilter. I have been quilting since 1980. In that time, not only have I had several careers, I tried every quilting fad that passed.

Just like I settled into my position as a mechanical engineer, I've settled into appliqué. It is an interesting juxtaposition. I get to capitalize on my attention to detail that is critical in engineering while also exercising the artist in me. I didn't like appliqué at first; however I've come to realize that it allows me to work in a world without restrictions. It is liberating.

I have pictures of quilts that trace my progression from a speed demon, one-a-weekend quilter to an "I can finish this kit" quilter; from a T-shirt-quilt-for-sale creator to a novice pattern creator; from a one-quilt-guild member to an annual quilt show organizer and two mini groups. Through my guild, I have been fortunate to have learned from quite a few well-known quilters. Each one has left me with a new outlook on quilting whether I enjoy their techniques or not.

My mind is never far from creating and that includes something as simple as color—whether it is stretching my limits of color from the traditional to eclectic or taking the time to dye my own fabric. Now when people ask me what my favorite color is, I can't answer because I can find a use or purpose for any color. Taking what seems offbeat or unwanted and giving it life within a quilt is rewarding to me.

Appliqué allows me the freedom to come up with an original design and see it evolve. Often, what I sketched at the outset is only a shadow of the quilt I create. I love that I am not tied to the design and, if I am inspired by a color or make a mistake, the quilt can be enhanced in a way that I never anticipated.

This quilt improvisation is hard to teach but I give it my best shot at Acorn Quilts, a local shop where I teach appliqué. I realize that every class has taught me a thing or two, a new tip or technique I have used to better myself as a quilter. That is one of the benefits of teaching.

I subscribe to the belief that you should always have five projects in process: one in design, one just being cut, one in the construction process, one almost complete, and one ready to quilt, so I have several options all vying for a bit of time.

Perhaps my favorite form of quilting is challenges. I love the idea of creating a design using a basic set of suggestions. That, and a friend, led me to enter this challenge and create a quilt that reflects so many of these parts of myself as a quilter—color, improvisation, and appliqué.

Inspiration and Design

Walking is therapeutic for me in many ways. When I walk, I let my head empty out and then let it fill on its own. This is the time I wrestle with ideas. I have to confess that too many times work issues take over, but it is those wonderful times when a quilt fills my head that leave me the most energized. That was true for this quilt. The use of the Basket block seemed like such a wide open category. Would it be traditional, artsy, totally distorted, or literal? During my walks, I sometimes thought of so many variations that when I finally put it on paper, it was almost exactly what I wanted.

"A-tisket, a-tasket, a green and yellow basket." Yes, that late nineteenth-century American nursery rhyme popped into my head and seemed ideal. What could I do with it? What style to use? How to portray it? I went through a whole list of options and finally decided on actually using the poem itself as the focus. This led to the fact that the words would have to be a major part of the design.

Almost immediately, I thought of the book plates that we used to put in the front of a book to list your name. I have always loved those. They seem so personal. But first, it was decision time—what genre? With the help of some clip art books, I focused on the font. You could spend a lifetime looking at fonts.

I checked out floral, art deco, art nouveau, vintage, and modern styles. There was no doubt that art nouveau won, hands down. Even narrowing the selection to art nouveau, there are so many free download public sites, I would need one that was interesting, not too hard to appliqué, and thick enough.

In my vision I knew I wanted a drop cap and I wanted to change colors in the background of the text. I saw several borders used in the book *Art Nouveau Design & Ornament.* This is one of the Dover Electronic Clip Art Books. All of these borders have overly large flowers. It was intimidating since I was thinking of using bold colors—black, red, orange, and yellow. I didn't know how bold it would be until I blew my drawing up to full-size and looked at the flowers. This was going to be a statement border.

With all of this said, I did not stray much from my initial drawing. Some of the placement changed and I added the white dots in the border to bring in just a bit of drama, but that was it. The fabric came from my stash except for the lined paper fabric and the black in the center. I can only hope that more of my designs will come together this well.

Techniques

This quilt offers three interesting techniques to highlight: text, contact paper patterns, and accent areas.

Using text can be fun in pattern-making and quilts. I have appliquéd text to quilts before, using the stan-

Appliqué allows me the freedom to come up with an original design and see it evolve.

dard plastic templates bought in the store for use on posters. In the past, I had also tried printing out a font and then cutting templates from the paper.

For this project, I found a free website that would allow me to download a font and use it as you would clip art. When sorting through all the art nouveau font choices, it was important to remember that I would be using needle-turn appliqué. The font would need to be fairly simple, yet represent the genre well. It would also need to have sturdy components.

When I finally found something I thought would be good and enlarged it to the size I needed, I was disappointed at how skinny it was. Using my quilting improvisation, I just added about another eighth of an inch to each letter, which was easy enough. Making templates that would hold up was the next step.

Clear contact paper would be the base for my patterns. In a project like this, there is a variety of very large, one-of-a-kind templates. I needed a method that would allow for creating templates that were going to be bigger than the normal template material and yet easy to transfer to fabric. I printed out the design on regular paper and then put clear contact paper on both sides. After I cut them out, they became almost indestructible and sturdy enough to draw around. Most of the templates in this quilt were done this way. I also used these patterns to play with the placement.

Lastly, my task as a designer was to decide how to add a bit of pizzazz by adding some accent elements that really finish the piece. This can be seen best by comparing this in-progress photo with the final quilt (page 10). At this point, two things are noticeable: the border looks flat and your eye is drawn to the dropped letter at the bottom of the quilt.

Editor's note: Permission secured from font designer for use in publication.

I decided to add the white circles to brighten the borders and carry the eye through the quilt. The last accent was adding red circles to the empty space in "I Dropped It." It was clear this space needed something but I wanted it to carry the eye through the space without distracting it. The red circles accomplished this nicely.

Quilting was difficult only in that it needed to be understated. The final step of this quilt was a cross-hatch background inside with 1" lines and the border with ½" lines. The flowers called for a little more interest so I finished them with free-motion quilting.

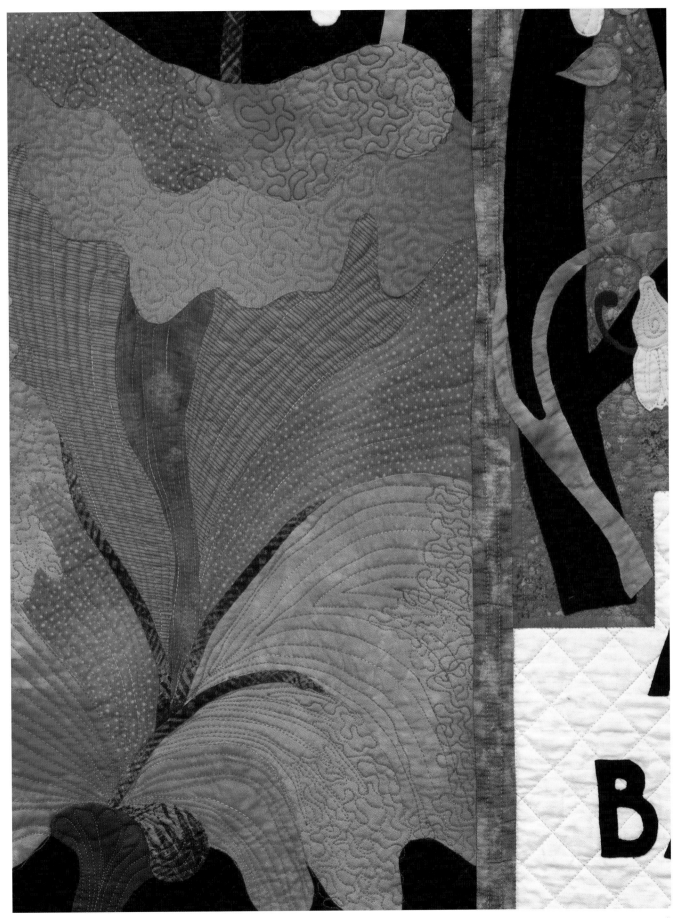

Second Place

Basket Case

52" x 52"

Photo by Mary Ann Taylor

Leona Harden
New Tazewell, Tennessee

I've been quilting for five years. My conversion from making a few dresses and handbags to making quilts for competition came about quite rapidly. One fall I decided to make my husband a green and white (Michigan State colors) lap quilt to cover up with and watch football. I sketched an original design on notebook paper and cut some triangle templates out of cardboard—that's how I thought it was done. I had it finished in a couple days. Of course, it was too short and looked a little cock-eyed. I thought, "I can do better than that!"

The next day, I was out purchasing my first quilt book and other tools I didn't even know existed! Six months later I was entering my first quilt show. I made so many quilts in the first three years, bringing one or two completely finished quilts to the guild meeting each month, one of the women said, "We should call you Turbo Quilter."

Inspiration and Design

I chose one of the baskets on the entry form I had picked up at the AQS Quilt Show in Knoxville, where I worked as a hostess. Jokingly, I had told a friend, "If I make one for this contest, I'd name it BASKET CASE." Three months went by before I took time from quilting for others to enter this contest. Staying in my "comfort zone" of the medallion style was the only hope I had to complete something show-worthy within the 30 days before the contest deadline. My love of bright colors, medallion-style design, and the thrill of a challenge, were the inspiration for this quilt.

Making the Quilt

I keep a photo diary of how I make my quilts, hopefully to learn from my mistakes. The following is taken from that diary.

Day 1: I'm very excited to begin! With pencils and paper in hand, I drew every kind of basket design I could find. Finally, I chose the basket design from the entry form. I traced around it, made eight copies enlarging them to fit in a circular fashion, and made freezer paper templates. I cut ¾" tall baskets out of freezer paper and enjoyed moving them around, trying one layout after another. I dove into my stash for more inspiration. When I pulled my collection of Caryl Bryer Fallert's Gradations by Bentarex that I bought at her Bryerpatch Studio, I knew these would be perfect!

Day 2: By the next afternoon, I had cut out 40, one-piece baskets from black fabric intended for reverse appliqué and I was very pleased with my efforts.

With no time to experiment with color pencils and markers, as I usually do when designing my original quilts, I combined this beautiful fabric and my imagination to speed the process. What most quilters would call a problem I prefer to call a challenge. In this case my challenge was I had very little of the Gradations lime green for fussy-cutting.

Day 3: I've never designed this fast before! More questions arise. I experimented with many color layouts on this "hands on" brainstorming project.

Day 4: I tried my favorite color for the background, with near disastrous results. It's hideous, right? Decision made: must use **black** and **brights**! My back is sore and my dear husband, Bill, almost set off the smoke alarm trying to use the toaster oven; my house is dirty, but I made progress!

Day 6: I used Dritz Liquid Stitch to fuse the triangle shapes to the baskets on a medium weight, non-woven interfacing by Pellon for reverse appliqué.

NOTE: A tiny line of Liquid Stitch does not adhere as well to Pellon interfacing as it does to cotton!

Day 8: I decided I needed a border. As I was drawing, my dear husband walked into the studio, took one look at my designs, and said, "Why don't you make stars?" When he tried to tell me how to draw stars, I patiently listened, tried his idea, then said, "Why don't you make yourself something to eat?"

The rest of the day was a blur of changing my mind a dozen times. I emailed pictures to my sister, Anna, and asked if she had any ideas to make it better.

Day 9: I had a great morning drafting, resulting in the final design. I've managed to connect the five large medallions as Anna suggested.

I emailed pictures to Anna and she was thrilled!

Basket Case took 26 days to complete. I'm not called "Turbo Quilter" for nothing!

When I complained that I wanted more movement, she said something about arrows.

Day 10: I placed some arrows in a rainbow fashion around the outside for a border and was very pleased with the results.

Day 14: After all the pieces had been liquid stitched in place and/or sewn down with my Janome 6600, I cut the black fabric out from behind the appliqués.

From the beginning of any quilting project, I think about how it is going to be quilted. This time, I don't have the luxury of time that it usually takes me to decide.

Day 15: I spent all day marking motifs in the medallion centers with Crayola Brand Washable markers on the medallions and Fons and Porter's mechanical chalk pen to mark on the black fabric in the borders with a basket design fitted in the arrows.

Day 17: I arranged to have the pets boarded and I made sure my machine and various threads were ready for a road trip to the Georgia Quilt Show. I plan on using any spare minute in the hotel to quilt. With the suitcases packed, I still have a little time to design a template for my quilting motif.

Day 20: Back home, I pieced together the back, loaded it and the wool batting onto my Tin Lizzie 18, and charged right into the quilting! After 15 minutes of quilting swirls in the top border, I took a good look at it and decided it looked like Quilting 101. It took four hours to rip it *out*.

Day 21: With the quilt already loaded and partially stabilized, I had to erase and re-mark the new quilting design. I wonder how many people will recognize the motif, let alone realize that the tiny baskets are a miniature of the large medallions. I decided to further embellish the 1½" baskets in the arrows and corners with Superior Threads Glitter Hologram Rainbow thread.

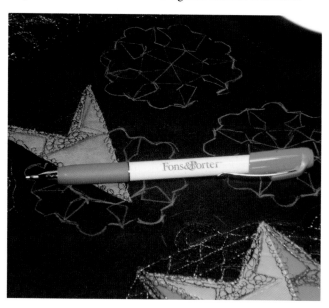

Day 25: Yes I am sweating, but confident at the same time, that I can get this done. Just one more embellishment, free-motion stitched with Superior Threads Razzle Dazzle by Ricky Tims after I took the quilt off the frame.

Day 26: As I pinned the binding around the quilt to make sure I had cut enough, my dear husband walked in and suggested I make the colors on the corners match up with the center. Now a three-hour job turned into a six-hour project!

NOTE: The binding was cut diagonally from a yard of Ombre Stripe, also from Caryl Bryer Fallert for Benartex.

Day 27: October 31, the day before the deadline, success!! The entry is on its way.

Third Place

Basket Weaver
60" x 59"

Michael Michalski
Brooklyn, New York

When people ask me what I do for a living, I say "I have two careers, as a theatrical wardrobe person and an artist." The first is my money job, the second is that which makes life fun. Backstage at a Broadway musical is a terrific situation, but after 25 years it does not give the thrill it once did. With my head working on a quilt design, the shows fly by as I look forward to sewing on my breaks and getting home to the current project at the end of the day.

Photo by Christopher Weston

Once the conversation turns from how much fun my job must be to what kind of artist I am, the inevitable questions begin: "How long does it make to make one?" and "How much does it cost to make one?" and on to some harder questions: "Why do you quilt?" and "What kind of quilter are you?"

My only answer for "Why quilt?" is that I feel compelled to. This is why I've come to call myself an artist. Quiltmaking is what I do but artist is how I feel. What kind of quilter am I is also hard to pin down. I've spent time at shows this year paying attention to the categories to see where I fit in. I'm definitely not pictorial, not quite traditional nor abstract, so I guess the best fit is innovative, which doesn't sound bad to me.

Being a quiltmaker and artist go hand in hand, but they feel like distinct personalities within me. A quiltmaker spends time keeping the traditional quilting values alive. Patterns from history provide continuity. Special attention is paid to accurate technique along with concerns about color, value, scale, line, and shape. Working solely in this realm doesn't necessarily do it for me.

An artist's primary goal is achieving visual excitement. They also use color, value, etc., but in a way to tug at your heart as well as your head. They may not win awards for technical merit but that is not their goal; they only seek in getting you to see things as they do. I too am trying to share how I perceive the world.

I find this right brain/left brain battle going on inside me. Being a perfectionist I am not happy if my workmanship is not more than merely acceptable. The demands of time constraint or just impatience lead

me to rush through things. Being so focused on those details feels very confining and I feel the need to break free from that and concentrate on fulfilling my vision. They speak of artist's passion, the drive and torment that pushes one to create sometimes to the point of madness. It is also the feeling of being alive, which is why I am proud to call myself a quilt artist.

Inspiration and Design

I found last year's Orange Peel contest such a fun challenge that I wanted to enter again this year, even though making a Basket quilt is not something that speaks to me. I wanted to get away from the block itself and just go with the idea of baskets in general.

As with last year, I started with a quick design to focus on the main characteristics of the block, purely as an exercise. I was happy with what I came up with but knew this was not what I would like to make for the contest.

The use of weaving spoke to me, so I started playing with what I could do to feature that. Baskets are airy constructions, with space inside, and gaps between the woven materials. I was also thinking about basket makers themselves. Maybe the quilt could be some kind of architectural construction to represent the shelves upon which wares would be presented for sale. I first worked with what looked like skewed walls in which niches would hold the baskets, but they came off weighty and baskets are about lightness.

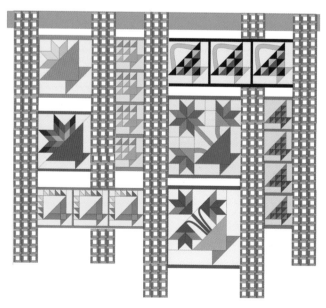

On to version 3. I started with a simple quilt block that reminded me of weaving. I have a (partially done) Double Wedding Ring where the football shapes are open spaces. I would leave the centers of the squares open in this manner to create more space. To me this evoked the outdoors; my basket weavers were selling their wares at an arts festival. (Renaissance Faire anyone?) These would be made into columns and supported by a girder type header, which acts as the sleeve. Between these columns would be the shelves.

As for the baskets themselves, why not take other blocks and adapt them into baskets, including more elements of weaving? I decided to stay within my comfort zone of circles and raided my idea folder for anything that would work.

I used some ideas that are recognizable as being used by well-known designers—RaNae Merrill's Mandalas, The QuiltMaven's Spiky Spirals, and Ricky Tims' Kool Kaleidoscopes, though that block did not make the final cut. I used a few things I had worked into quilts

My only answer for "Why quilt?"
is that I feel compelled to.

before such as my Mid-Century Modern Star (upper left in finished quilt). I filled in with a Mariner's Compass, a Dresden Plate, and a Lone Star (oh my!). Some blocks were big and dynamic, some small and fussy. I wanted a wide range and felt I was on to something .

The baskets were all foundation pieced on Ricky Tims' Poly Stable Stuff. I decided to use the same design on all the handles to tie the disparate styles of the baskets together. The background needed some detail. By quilting the background, then applying the grid, it would float on top. The baskets and handles were quilted individually before being stitched on. I chose different quilting styles for each basket to emphasize their uniqueness.

Technique

The open columns proved to be more of a challenge than I had imagined. I started with strips twice as wide as the finished bars would be (cut at 1" to finish at ½").

I ran these through the bias machine (invaluable in making this quilt), though you could just fold one edge to the center line and press a crease. These strips were cut to the proper length (2" including seam allowance).

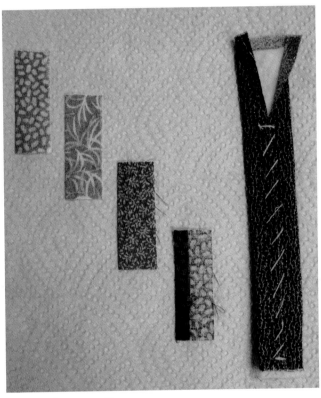

Strips ready to assemble

The strips were stitched into an open square.

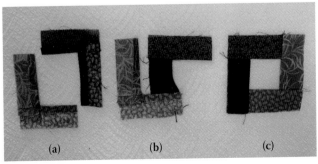

(a)   (b)   (c)

a. Partially assembled   b. Pinning the next seam   c. Finished square

The columns were backed with strips of fabric (cut at 2" for the horizontals and center column, 1" for the sides) basted around strips of batting. The wide strips were applied to the back and quilted.

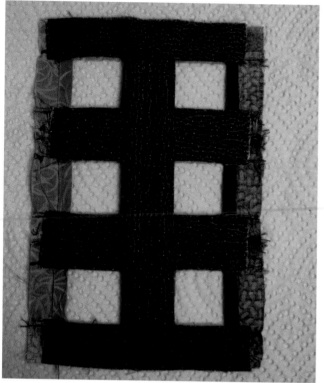

Back of column

Front of column

When the Basket blocks were attached to the columns and hung from the header, I discovered the spaces I had left between the blocks were too big. More lattice was added, but I was still afraid it would sag over time. One morning in bed while puzzling this out as I awoke, it hit me—why not back it with net? (I must have seen this someplace and filed it away to pop out when needed.) So the lattice strips were appliquéd and now I had a stable and square quilt.

I love how these rows of open squares turned out. I think I'll try using them as sashing in another project—Jacob's Ladder perhaps?

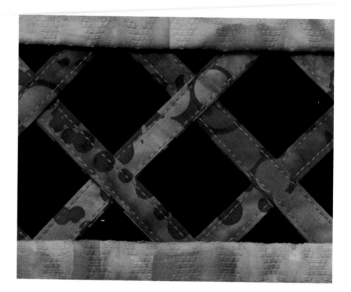

Fourth Place

Sycamore Bark Baskets

51½" x 51½"

Marilyn R. Smith
Columbia, Missouri

Like so many other quilters, I began making doll clothes with a needle and thread. Soon I convinced my mom to let me use her old treadle sewing machine. When I was eight years old, a neighbor suggested that I might like to join 4-H, which became my only out-of-school activity until I started high school. I was the kind of child who never asked for help, so I struggled through my sewing projects, learning through my many mistakes.

Photo by Cheryl Morris

I continued to sew many of my clothes throughout high school and college and when I got married I made my bridesmaid dresses. It was only natural to make clothing for my husband, son, and daughter, but for some reason, I just wasn't inspired to quilt.

My husband was killed in a tragic accident in 1999 and I stopped sewing. I just couldn't find any joy in it. In 2004 I was with my neighbor when she stopped at a quilt shop and it was like a door had opened for me. I signed up for a Pineapple Lone Star paper-piecing class taught by Sharon Rexroad. I pieced all the diamond units but didn't complete it until 2006. I began borrowing my neighbor's quilt books and magazines to search for border ideas. I was astonished at the quilts being made. I was hooked!

I never earned a blue ribbon at my county fair for my sewing, but at the 2008 AQS Quilt Show & Contest in Paducah I was shocked to learn that my appliquéd quilt JOY had won a blue ribbon. It has been my goal to have one of my quilts hang at The National Quilt Museum so I am so pleased and honored that Sycamore Bark Baskets will hang there and be part of the traveling exhibit.

Inspiration

My entry into the Burgoyne Surrounded NQOF contest was not accepted for the exhibit and I really wanted to try again. It was on an August family canoe trip on the Jack's Fork River in Missouri's beautiful Ozarks that my idea came to me. We frequently stopped along the river and as I searched along the gravel bar, I began to see pieces of sycamore bark. It was so beautifully organic in form. The pieces had little holes in them and seemed to have a "backing" that followed the contours of the bark.

On the way home I decided that perhaps I could adapt the form of the sycamore bark into triangles for a basket. Once home I realized that it was possible! I searched my stash for fabrics and was on my way, with little more than two months until the November 1 deadline!

Design and Techniques

Making Basket Triangles

First I divided my background fabric into triangular quadrants, marking it with a water-soluble marker. I divided each quadrant into triangles to mirror the Basket pattern. I left a square in the middle of the background and plenty of room for the handles. I made a plastic template to fit the marked triangles.

I decided to back each piece of bark with pink that I thought went well with my coffee-colored solid background and was prevalent in my inspiration fabric. I applied Wonder Under to the various pieces of my curved piecing fabrics. Using the triangle template, I marked the triangles onto the curved piecing fabrics and cut out the triangles with my rotary cutter.

I free-hand drew the bark outline on the paper backing of the Wonder Under, randomly adding a hole or two to each piece. I kept in mind that each piece of bark should be at least ¼" smaller than the pink back-

ground triangle. Using my tiny sharp scissors, I carefully cut out each piece of bark differently—nothing in nature is identical.

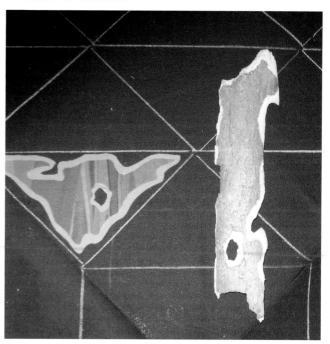

I used the same triangle template to mark triangles on the pink fabric. I fused the cut-out bark pieces onto the pink fabric, backed the pink fabric with Wonder Under, and cut out the pink triangles with my rotary cutter. I used my tiny sharp scissors to echo the outline of the bark pieces on the pink fabric and fused the completed bark pieces to the background.

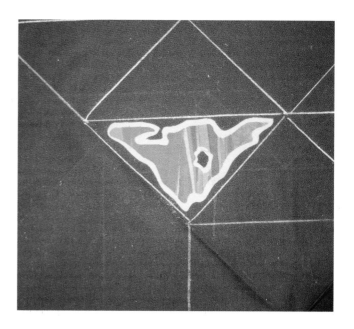

I developed my own technique and called it Captured Raw Edge Fused Appliqué.

Handles

For the basket handles, I tried various ideas and finally settled on a bark handle, making the pieces in the same way I had made the bark triangles.

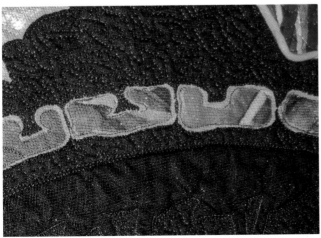

At this point I did not know how I was going to fill the large area outside the bark handles. Last April at the Paducah show I had purchased some stencils and one of them just happened to look like a sycamore leaf. I decided that I wanted to try some new techniques on this quilt and one of those was stenciling with paints.

I stenciled the leaves onto the pink fabric, using Pebeo Setacolor Paints and a small stencil brush. I painted them in layers, using some of the same colors as in the inspiration fabric and adding a second layer of iridescent paints. I heat-set the paints, backed the fabric with Wonder Under, and cut the leaves out, leaving a ¼" pink edging to the leaves. I then tried different arrangements and fused the leaves to the quilt.

Filling the Baskets

To fill the baskets, I decided to try trapunto. I drew a symmetrical tree, made a template, and traced the outline onto the quilt. I pinned batting to the back and stitched the outline of the tree with water-soluble thread. I then carefully cut away the excess batting and my trapunto was complete. It was subtle, organic, and fit perfectly with the theme of my quilt.

Captured Raw Edge Fused Appliqué

I began to explore ways of securing the fused pieces to the background—something other than machine appliqué. After much thought I decided to try tulle. The tulle could overlay the entire appliqué part of the quilt. I could machine stitch closely around the edge of each bark and leaf motif and the motif would be captured within the tulle! I had just developed a new technique! The raw edges would be captured to prevent them from moving and fraying and the small amount of stitch in the ditch over the pieced edges of the motif would hold it in place.

Tulle requires special handling. Use a cool iron when ironing the tulle overlay. If your iron is too hot it will melt the tulle. (Don't ask me how I know this.)

Tulle is easy to snag on your sewing machine and can be torn. When I was free-motion machine quilting my quilt, I tore the tulle and had to repair it several times before I finally discovered that one of my thread guides was snagging it. I covered the guide with tape and solved that problem. As I finished quilting each area, I covered it with Glad® Press'n Seal

to protect it while I worked in other areas. That way I knew it would be protected from snags and tears. Tulle in itself is strong, but a snag will lead to tears... and tears!

Finishing

I sewed a line of handmade piping around the perimeter of the central basket design to cover the edges of the tulle overlay and added the framed border of the inspiration fabric. I loved it! My top was finally complete by the end of September. I knew without a doubt I could quilt and finish it in time.

I sandwiched my quilt with 80/20 cotton batting and the coffee solid used in the front. I used brown thread in the needle and pink thread in the bobbin. I love for my quilting to show on the back; in fact, I sometimes like the back better than the front of the quilt!

I free-motion stitched around the bark pieces, and meander quilted around the trapunto to make the trapunto stand out. I followed the veins of the leaves and meander quilted around them. On the framing background I used a transparent thread in the needle and did a type of McTavishing. All of the quilting was done free-motion.

I then focused on the edge of the quilt. I began by blocking the quilt and then squaring it up. I have always admired Sharon Schamber's quilts with hand-turned corded edging and chose to make a simple looped edging to mirror the many arcs in my quilt and especially the arched handles of the baskets. After the edging was on I added a bias binding and then hand sewed the binding to the back of the quilt.

I blocked the quilt once more to ensure it was square. I had met the deadline with three days to spare!

Fifth Place

Basket Case Flowers
66" x 64"

Photo by Rebecca Cox

Ann L. Petersen
Aurora, Colorado

One of my earliest memories of sewing is shopping with my mother for fabric for an Easter dress. Picking out an embroidered organdy with purple roses and anticipating the beautiful dress I would soon have is a very happy memory and just one of the many gifted moments my mother, Patricia Lucore, gave me. She has always been my hero and role model. She exemplified how to live a creative life and how to always look for ways to give back to others—a key part of my desire to teach others the joys of quilting.

I have been teaching since 1998, shortly after I started to work at the local quilt shop. My coworkers encouraged me to teach, even though I doubted whether I would ever be good enough. The encouragement of the people I worked with made every step I took as a quilter much better than the one before. The store closed in 2011 and losing the support and daily camaraderie of those people has been hard.

Three things inspired my work and brought me back to quilting from general crafts and garment sewing in the early 90s. The first is a love of the geometrical beauty of quilt designs. Traditional patchwork has always held great appeal to me, and in modern combinations and colors gives me wide range of design to play with and enjoy. The second is color. I believe that the palette quilters have is one of the richest and most diverse in all artistic pursuits. The wonderful things that happen with color when a printed fabric is viewed close up and far away and with other printed fabrics seems magical to me. So much texture and design and color can never be boring. Playing with the geometrical designs and the color is wonderful.

The third is the sculptural beauty added to a quilt with the addition of quilting. Using differing threads, many different quilting designs and contrast of line and curve can add a literal new layer of delight in a quilt, much of it only seen as one draws closer to the work. This simple act of stitches holding three layers together becomes a level of beauty that can take my breath away. You can see all three inspirations in all my work—it is highly geometric and pieced; uses as many fabrics as possible to accomplish washes of color and contrast; and has lots and lots of machine quilting.

Since the closing of the quilt store, I am very much enjoying my forced "retirement." I am much more free to concentrate on making each quilt as complex as I wish. My days usually revolve around quilting, being with quilting friends, or planning new quilting designs. I teach several times a month and occasionally give presentations at guild meetings, but mostly I quilt. I seem to always look eagerly forward to the next project, although I am usually very tired of a particular quilt by the time it is finished. Putting it away for several weeks or sending it off to a show usually makes me like it again the next time I see it.

Inspiration and Design

When first challenged to use the Basket block for a new quilt, I really had no new ideas for such a traditional block. Then one night while trying to get to sleep, the idea came to me that instead of making a basket of flowers, I could make flowers of baskets. This appealed to my sense of humor, sort of a visual pun. I played for a while with different configurations and decided to turn the blocks with their bases toward the centers and use the handles for flower petals.

The biggest challenge was deciding just how to implement the design. After some experimenting, I decided to piece the main part of four baskets and appliqué the handles and bases, as well as an additional four baskets. The pieced baskets were placed on top of the appliquéd ones with the blocks making up each large flower. Appliquéd handles and bases were added to all blocks.

All piecing seams were pressed open to avoid too much bulk along the raw edges when machine appliquéing them. My decision to use different programmed stitches for the appliqué was to provide a more dense stitch to hold down the raw edges. I fused strips of fusible web to the edges of the baskets and then trimmed off the outside seam allowances from the pieced sections and fused my sections together to make a basket that I could place in various positions on my top.

The best design decision came toward the end with the lucky find of a batik fabric with a large-scale repeating design in the right shade of green. This leafy print matched in theme, scale, and color and offered up a ready-made quilting design. I added the fabric on just two sides and then quilted the design into the other two sides. Quilting the border was fun and added great impact.

Fabric quilting

Quilted border fabric

Technique

I started the quilt background by cutting a few rectangles from all my green batiks and played with placement from dark to light. Greens encompass a wide spectrum, from blue-greens to yellow-greens and even dark yellows, that can make it difficult to decide where to place some fabrics. I really like the resulting look, however. An absolutely smooth transition can look too perfect and I want the variety with pops of light and shifts of color adding luminosity. Using all batiks, with their fun stamped designs, gave the piece the look of a sun-dappled flowerbed.

The encouragement of the people I worked with made every step I made as a quilter much better than the one before.

Trapunto made the flowers come forward visually, with two layers of polyester batting on each large flower and one layer on the leaves and small flowers. This was first stitched behind each flower in the ditch with water-soluble thread.

Trapunto before trimming

Technique sample

I carefully trimmed away the excess batting from the edges and layered the quilt with cotton batting. I quilted the quilt as I normally would. The water-soluble thread washed away while wetting the quilt for blocking when I was done.

I did a sample of this technique to make sure it worked. (The sample also has an area where I practiced dry brushing the paint and quilting a honeybee motif I had designed.) Because of the extra layers of batting behind the flowers, I quilted those areas much less densely. The trapunto actually shows much more dimension on the back of the quilt than the front. The top is made entirely of batiks, which have a very high thread count, and so most of the definition is on the back, which is a commercial cotton print. My sample has a batik back, resulting in more definition showing on the front.

A very small amount of acrylic fabric paint was added to the quilt dragonflies and butterfly. After they were quilted in, I felt they needed more prominence so I took a dry painting brush, lightly touched it to the paint, wiped it on a paper towel until just a hint of color was coming off of the brush, and then repeated until I felt the effect was strong enough. The paints had a small amount of glitter in them. I also used this technique to add a little shading to stems where they disappeared behind leaves, flowers, etc., giving it a small amount of shading and definition.

The largest pink flower had a polyester ribbon yarn fused on the handles, and then a herringbone hand stitch was done over the top with perle cotton. A few glass beads were sewn to a few of the flowers for a touch of sparkle. I hand sewed beads with a nylon beading thread after the quilt was finished, burying my threads.

Finalist

Spice Market

52" x 52"

Sherri Bain Driver
Northglenn, Colorado

I started sewing when I was eight years old, making clothing and household items. Through the years I have done lots of different kinds of needlework, including cross-stitch, smocking, needlepoint, and crewel, but I always loved sewing best. I started quilting as a way to use scraps left over from clothing construction, thinking it would be a thrifty hobby. Silly me! My first quilt was truly a scrap quilt, but I soon gathered a stash of new fabrics and, of course, that continues today.

Photo by Robert K. Driver

I became involved in several quilt guilds and smaller quilting bees. I'm still a member of a bee I joined in 1987! Our monthly get-togethers are more social now, revolving around pot lucks, but we also have an annual retreat.

What began as a fun hobby has turned into a career for me. I've worked for 12 years on the staffs of several quilt magazines, and really love what I do. I get to look at beautiful quilts and fabrics every day...and that's my job!

With a busy job it can be hard to find time to make quilts, but I'm lucky to have a dedicated sewing room and a family who understands that quilting makes me very happy. I spend time in my sewing room every day, shuffling fabrics, evaluating a quilt in progress on the design wall, doodling in a sketchbook, or reading about a new technique.

Inspiration and Design

My favorite quilts are based on traditional designs, but with a twist, so I've been interested in the NQOF annual challenge since it was first introduced in 1994. Whether or not I finish a quilt by each year's challenge deadline, I sketch designs with each selected block, pull fabrics from my stash, and consider making a quilt for the contest. Even thinking about the blocks helps expand my quilting horizons in some way. This contest has inspired me to push my design and construction skills, some years working with familiar favorite blocks and sometimes playing with blocks that I've never used before.

When I was just beginning to make quilts, I discovered and fell in love with ikat fabrics. These fabrics are made with warp and/or weft yarns (threads) that are tied in bundles and hand dyed to create various designs that appear when the fabric is woven. Twenty-five years of collecting ikats has given me a huge closet overflowing with fabrics from all over the world—some purchased in exotic places and others found at local quilt, fabric, or thrift shops. I have found ikats in the form of new and used clothing or other household textiles. (Some of the patches in SPICE MARKET were cut from ikat napkins that a friend found at a household goods store.) I love to design quilts that showcase the unique nature of these fabrics.

I was initially concerned that ikats might be too coarsely woven to use in quilts and that they might present problems with construction, but I forged ahead anyway, and have been pleasantly surprised with the final results of the quilts I have made with ikats. They are certainly unique. Using ikats has continued to be the basis for the quilts I've made for this annual contest.

I'm drawn to medallion-style and circular designs, and wanted to see what Basket blocks would look like drafted around a circle. My initial graph-paper sketch looked interesting, really more like a feathered star than baskets, but I liked the idea that you had to look hard to find baskets.

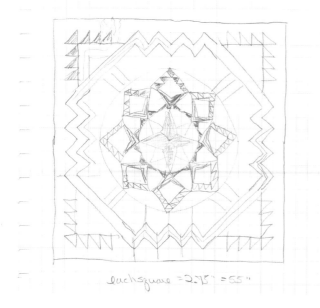

each square = 2.75" = 55"

Before I fine-tune a drawn design, I audition fabrics by pinning them to my design wall. I'm looking for a group of fabrics that feel unified, yet have an interesting variety of colors and shapes with different scale motifs, and also have value differences to define patch shapes. As I make the quilt top, I continue to audition fabrics. I often find a quilt design going in a direction I hadn't expected, and it's fun to just see where that leads.

Technique

I sketched a rough drawing on graph paper, and when I was happy with the design and a group of fabrics I was ready to get started. SPICE MARKET was made in sections—the background and the center circle.

The circular center design was drafted full-size onto Sulky Totally Stable. This material is similar to freezer paper, but is much more flexible, making it easier to manipulate under the sewing machine. I used the Amazing Rays tool (similar to a huge compass) developed by Renae Haddadin to draft the various circles, make even divisions, and to draw registration marks for the rest of the lines.

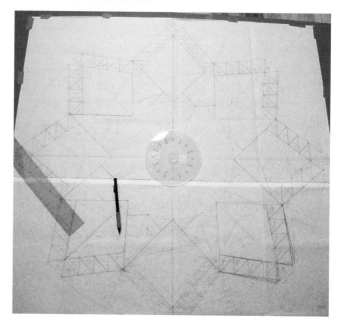

The baskets were more challenging to draft than I had expected, so there was a lot of trial and error (and erasing!) before I completed the paper pattern. Theoretically, duplicate shapes in the pattern should be exactly the same, but, unless you are absolutely perfect at drafting and cutting the pattern pieces apart, they are not interchangeable. To be sure the pattern could be reconstructed correctly, I numbered each piece before I cut up the pattern. Some pieces were used as foundations for paper piecing, and others were used as iron-on templates.

I started quilting as a way to use scraps left over from clothing construction, thinking it would be a thrifty hobby. Silly me!

Most of the circular center was constructed at a Bee retreat. I hadn't chosen all the fabrics for this part of the quilt, so I had to make some quick decisions about which fabrics to pack for the long weekend. I filled the suitcase with a bunch of fabrics that I thought could work, including lights and darks, plus fabrics with large- and small-scale motifs that all "played well together." I was determined to complete the center during the retreat, using those fabrics. I know if I had pieced this at home with 10 times as many choices, it would have taken 10 times as long to make it!

The background was made with traditional piecing using rotary-cut patches and some patches cut using templates. Sizes for rotary cutting and drafted templates were determined by looking at that small graph paper drawing and keeping in mind that each graph-paper square represents 2¾". Fabrics were auditioned before cutting, and then cut patches were arranged on the design wall. Fabrics were added, discarded, and rearranged until I was satisfied with the composition. Traditional piecing was used for the background, with lots of set-ins for the zigzag border.

After both the center and background were constructed, the circle was appliquéd onto the background using a narrow strip of fabric (loosely woven, but not cut on the bias) eased on to cover the raw edges of the circle. The portion of the background under the circle was cut away, and then I carefully removed the Totally Stable from the back of the pieced circle.

Finalist

Basket Weave
73½" x 73½"

Photo by Neal Erickson

Ann Feitelson
Montague, Massachusetts

Ronna Erickson
Amherst, Massachusetts

Meet Ronna (on the right)

I am a process-oriented person and enjoy all aspects of quilting. I especially enjoy exploring new techniques and playing with the flow of value and color in arranging quilt blocks. The enjoyment of arranging color and pattern in a quilt is similar to that which I had when I worked in textile design in the 1970s. (I have a BFA in textiles/surface pattern design from Syracuse University, College of Visual and Performing Arts).

Currently, my time and creative attention are split among a variety of activities. In addition to the time spent at my job building equipment for radio astronomy (I also have a degree in astrophysics), I have recently taken up playing classical guitar. The study of music and the time I spend practicing has put a significant dent into the time I have for quilting, but I still enjoy a variety of fiber arts, such as weaving, bobbin lace, and knitting, along with quilting.

Although I tend to be a perfectionist in producing my final product, it is the process of discovery and working with my hands that I enjoy, no matter what field of endeavor. I have been quilting for approximately 12 years.

Meet Ann (on the left)

Although Ronna and I enjoy many similar things, I am more product-oriented. With quilting and knitting, I'm aiming for the satisfaction of the completed object. I don't tend to work on more than one thing at a time. My training in art school, and my experience as a painter of landscape and still life during my twenties, informs my goals as a quilter. The New York Studio School, where I studied in the 1970s, emphasized persistence in seeking the elusive goal of portraying spatial forces, and being truthful to the flux of the perceptive moment.

There were no small goals in its instruction, only big goals: to say it all, to be passionate about what you saw. That vision still inspires me to create quilts with big movements and shapes, with a push and pull of linear, planar, and volumetric tensions; to make something fantastic and bold, not equivocal. Although I certainly used color as a painter and as a knitter, I don't think it was until I started quilting—about 12 years ago —that I truly understood how to mine color for its potential of rich sensation. Although color is always appealing as pure emotion, pure joy, it truly comes alive in the multiple combinations quiltmaking provides. I just love color!

The Collaboration: Ronna

This quilt was a particular challenge for me because I suffered a severe injury (a fractured thoracic vertebra) in January 2011 and needed major surgery in April to keep a shard of bone from severing my spinal cord. There were times at the beginning of the project when I was not sure I would have the energy to work on the quilt at all.

During this difficult time, Ann visited me in the hospital, stayed overnight with me when my husband had to leave town to attend his mother's funeral, spent afternoons visiting me during my convalescence, and accompanied me on walks that were necessary for my recovery. Ann's loyal companionship and persistence in keeping me involved in the process during the initial phases of this quilt helped a great deal in bringing me back to the world of normal activities. It was not as fully equal a collaboration as some of the other quilts we have worked on together, as Ann did the lion's share of the sewing.

It is a tribute to the friendship that we share for Ann to call this quilt a collaboration. Her energy to keep me involved was instrumental in keeping me moving on the path to a full recovery while my input and what energy I could spare helped to keep this quilt moving along to its inclusion in this year's New Quilts from an Old Favorite contest.

Inspiration and Design

Ronna

When Ann mentioned that the block for this year's contest was Baskets, as a weaver, the first thing that came to my mind was basket weave. This became our concept for the quilt. Would we somehow imitate weaving, with color strips, and have a border of baskets? Would we have a central basket that transformed into a basket weave pattern? In the end, we decided to interweave Basket blocks themselves, without an additional woven component. The Basket blocks seemed to "point" the way with their triangle shapes and we thought to control the movement in the quilt using that visual cue to guide the viewer's attention.

Ann

Woven stripes and plaids seemed fitting to connote woven baskets. I love how they express the nature of a real, woven basket. I cut the baskets and handles both on the bias and parallel to the lines of stripes and plaids, varying them just for the pleasure of seeing the many ways (horizontal, vertical, diagonal) they could align with the shapes of the block.

Technique: Ann

Most of my quilts use color in sequences and combination of sequences. For these Basket blocks, I combined sequences of five solids with sequences of five woven plaids or striped fabrics. For example, five solids running from yellow through orange to red, combined with five plaids shifting from yellow to green to blue, resulted in a set of 25 blocks, each plaid appearing with each solid; each solid appearing with each plaid. All are different combinations yet all are interrelated. I knew that if I made them fairly small (they're 4" square) and arranged them so that sets of 25 intersected and interwove, something interesting would happen. But I certainly didn't know what at the start!

In early summer, bright clear colors seemed appropriate to the brilliant sunny season. (I always have some kind of color feeling about season and weather.) I started generating sets of 25 Basket blocks. Ronna first came to my house when I had three sets completed and she took some fabric home to sew some blocks. I kept making sets, arranging them in different ways. She came back again when I had several more sets, and we were able, together, to create a promising composition.

It is a tribute to the friendship that we share for Ann to call this quilt a collaboration.

Although her actual time spent sewing was small, her clear vision of where the composition ought to go, of where to put all the blocks that were multiplying at my house, was extremely valuable for bringing the quilt to completion.

Interweaving many groups of 25, which are themselves comprised of two shifting sequences of five colors, is boggling to the eye in a way that we find fascinating and satisfying. It overloads the eye and the mind with information, some of it conflicting; resolution is impossible. We know that a viewer of the quilt may find it difficult to see the sets of 25; even the creators find it challenging to decode it now.

There are a total of about nine different sets of 25 blocks in the quilt, but there are some partial sets where irregular areas needed to be filled in. To help decode the quilt's color groups, notice the directions of the basket handles; when they face the same direction, they are part of the same group; when the direction changes, that indicates a new set of blocks.

To illustrate the concept of the 25 color-sequenced blocks, I made 50 new ones (maybe there is another Basket quilt in my future!). Here they are, as separate sets.

And here, they are combined in three different ways.

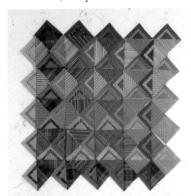

The number of ways they can be combined is infinite: a set of 25 could be arranged as a square, a diamond, or a parallelogram. Another set of 25 could intersect fully or partially; centered, or off-center. The possibilities of working with groups of interrelated colors are fascinatingly endless—or is it endlessly fascinating?

Pharaoh's Tombs

50" x 50"

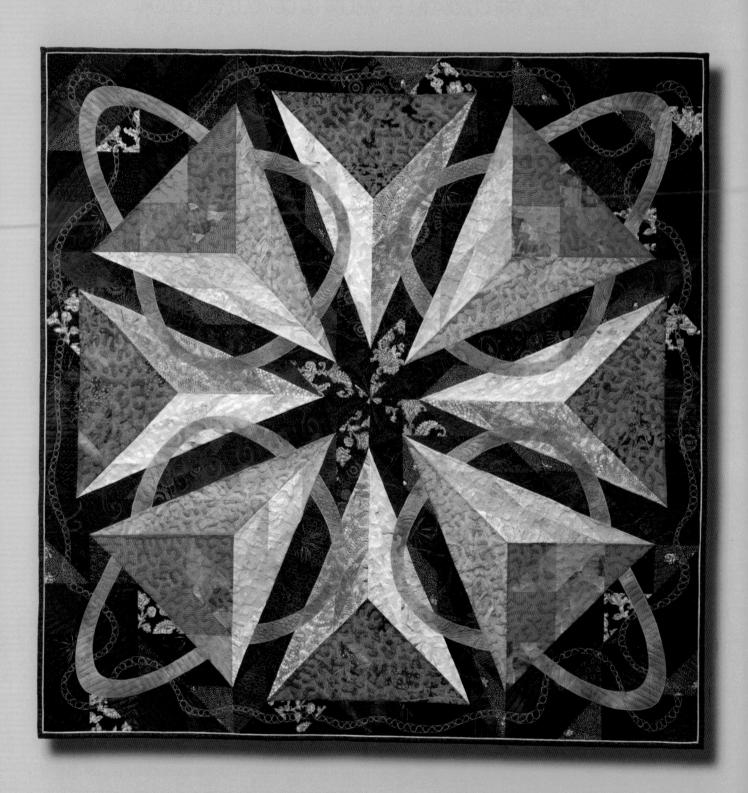

Photo Amy J. Graber

Julia Graber
Brooksville, Mississippi

My interest in quiltmaking was sparked in my early twenties while working as a clerk at my parents' fabric store, The Clothes Line, in Dayton, Virginia. I learned to make my own clothes in home economics classes. While working at the store in the evenings, I would see many fabrics and dream of putting quilts together.

I began making utility quilts in my early twenties, not the art quilts that I've learned to enjoy now. I pieced and tied several of those before I married. After marrying, I began to experiment more and more, with each quilt becoming more challenging than the last.

In time, I joined a few of my sisters in a round-robin project. We each made a quilt center and passed it on to the next sister to add to it. In the end, we each had a quilt. Next, I taught a class of high-school girls how to piece quilt blocks. Those two events taught me a lot about quiltmaking. I began to spearhead projects for my church's sewing circle, which involved making quilts for charity. I have also taught several quiltmaking classes in my home, and my love for the craft has grown with each quilt made.

I come from a family of seven sisters and one brother. Each year, we have a retreat that not only includes our family, but also our nieces and nephews and extended family. For an entire week, we sew and quilt, make baskets or scrapbooks, and talk and laugh together. We take our current projects and work on them, learning and gaining inspiration from each other.

The Family's Farmer's Delight Quilts

This FARMER'S DELIGHT quilt was made by my g.reat-aunt Ocky, circa 1903. Notice the two circles of triangles around the center star in each block.

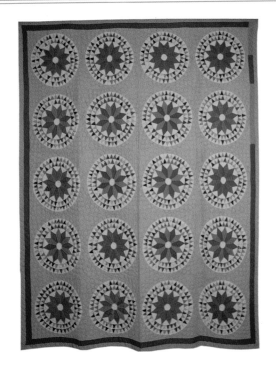

FARMER'S DELIGHT, made by Octavia Early, Dayton, Virginia

Our grandmother was a very creative quilter. She made this green quilt for my parents. Father yearned for one with two rings of triangles, so he paid Grandmother to make him the blue one.

FARMER'S DELIGHT quilts, made by Vera Early Heatwole, Dayton, Virginia

Of the 15 FARMER'S DELIGHT bed-size quilts that Grandmother made, this is the only one that she sold. Years later it was spotted at an antique shop and my brother Oren Jr. bought it as a surprise for his wife, Cheryl.

These quilts have inspired many of us to make our own. My sister Polly redrafted the pattern for paper piecing and made this one in plums and greens, adding the swags and appliqué.

FARMER'S DELIGHT, made by Polly Yoder, Greenwood, Delaware

Another sister, Barbara, added Mariner's Stars to hers and used portions of the triangle rings for a scalloped border.

FARMER'S DELIGHT, made by Barbara Cline, Bridgewater, Virginia

I come from a family of seven sisters and one brother. It thrills us now to see some of our daughters take up the craft [of quilting].

My niece Afton made the center block of this five generation FARMER'S DELIGHT quilt. The other blocks were made by her mother, Jolene; her grandmother, June; her great-grandmother, Margaret; and her great-great grandmother, Vera (my grandmother).

So, what more could I do than to make my own FARMER'S DELIGHT? I chose red and white fabrics and made a small version with a contemporary look and called it FAMILY CIRCLE.

Five generation FARMER'S DELIGHT

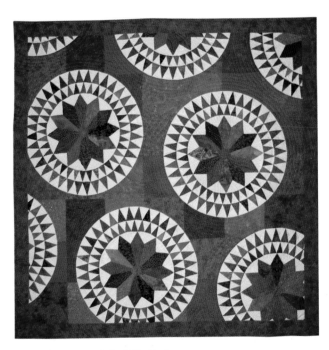

FAMILY CIRCLE, made by Julia Graber

So the tradition is being carried on. It thrills us now to see some of our daughters take up the craft. I feel so blessed to be part of my family. Visit me on my blog http://juliagraber.blogspot.com to see other quilts and activities of my life.

Inspiration and Design

I love the challenge of the annual New Quilts from an Old Favorite contest. This year I used EQ7 in my designing. I liked this fresh modern look of the Bas-kets in the Courthouse design, but my family didn't think it to be a winner.

I went on trying and naming several more designs including these:

Potential Basket in the Courthouse design

Potential Rows of Baskets design

Potential Basket in Baskets design

Potential Blue Baskets design

It was the Blue Baskets design that went on to became PHARAOH'S TOMBS. My sister Emily thought the baskets looked more like pyramids, and suggested the name.

So many people have asked, "How did you make that?" And really it was very simple. I took a simple LeMoyne Star layout and placed my Basket block into each diamond and square. Too many handles overloaded the design and took away from the overall effect, so I only added handles to 12 of the baskets.

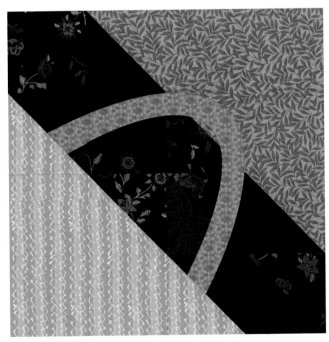

Traditional LeMoyne Star block

Basket block adapted to the LeMoyne Star diamond shape

My Basket block

Finalist

Fibonacci Nebula

59" x 50"

Patricia Hobbs
Macomb, Illinois

Photo John K. Hobbs

Let me preface this story with, "No, I am not older than dirt!" However, my folks did own a black Model A car. It had woven straw seats. I sat in the back with my older brother with suitcases between us (to avoid any arguments that might occur). On long trips, I would pick at the hole on the corner of the front seat. It was great fun to unweave the straw and then weave it back again until mother caught me. That should have been a clue that I would end up making fiber art.

I actively began making quilts at age fourteen. English paper piecing caught my attention. Then many baby quilts for friends were made. In college, I made a small wallhanging in weaving class in 1969.

When I retired after 34 years of teaching art, I began moving more toward quilting, leaving watercolor painting to become second place. I like crazy quilting because there are no rules and art quilts because they may be painted or manipulated in many different ways. For me, it is all about the designing process. Designing is a thread that runs through our family's talents.

My mother's family comes from a long line of seamstresses and quilters. The quilt on my childhood bed was a red and white star pattern. The "Hap" was a favorite around our home. This was a blanket made of rectangles of wool suiting, layered, and tied. Its conception and necessity came out of the Depression Era. Mother gave me an unfinished one when I was first married. None of the rectangles' corners matched and there were a few moth holes in it by the time I decided to finish it in 2007. Even though Mom had passed on, I felt like we had worked on this quilt together.

I have been working on a series of genealogy quilts for a few years. I am currently working on a Chero-kee Red Paint or Hawk clan quilt as a tribute to my husband's heritage. Hopefully, it will be in a National Holiday Quilt Show in Tahlequah, Oklahoma, that commemorates the anniversary of the signing of the Cherokee Nation Constitution in 1839. I wanted to put the Cherokee Nation's official government seal on my quilt. The official permission came with the greeting, "Osiyo" or "Hello, Mrs. Hobbs."

The quilting world leads me in new directions with exciting opportunities and new friends. This Goethe quote sums up my success in the quilting world: "Progress has not followed a straight ascending line, but a spiral with rhythms of progress and retrogression. . . ."

My hope is that my skills will improve with each quilt I make. Right now there are plans for seventeen new quilts on the drawing board, but there will always be room left for making charity quilts or quilts made for fundraising for a worthy cause.

Inspiration and Design

The National Quilt Museum inspired me to make this quilt with the New Quilts from an Old Favorite-Baskets challenge. All of my Prairie Quilters guild members will testify that I love a challenge and to show/share my quilts.

When I typed "baskets" into the computer, Keith Mackay's fractal *Underwater Basket Weaving* popped up and caught my eye. I could just see little baskets in his design. Politely asking permission is the correct thing to do copyright-wise, and it is easy. When I emailed Keith, he seemed so upbeat and happy to have been the inspiration for my quilt. Keith said:

> Thanks so much for asking for permission. Sure, you can use that image. I have no idea how you would go about making it into a quilt, but what do I know? I would enjoy seeing the result so please send me a picture when you have it finished.

> I have been approached before by a quilter. It was a while ago and I don't remember in which image they were interested. Must be something about fractals and quilts . . . .

Finding the correct scale of prints for the baskets was the challenge. I wanted it to "break-up" into the background, but the basket shape could not totally disappear. Since I live in a small town, I can't go out and buy exactly what I need to work on a project. My answer was to paint PFD (prepared for dying) fabric with watered down Azure Blue Dye-Na-Flow paint. I tried to make it a light to dark ombre.

The most enjoyable part was sewing on the glass beads. Several shades of amber-colored beads were mixed in a bowl and randomly sewn onto the quilt. The beads were to create a stardust effect in outer space. However, the iridescent gossamer chiffon, metallic threads, and bead embellishments made the quilt difficult to photograph.

Technique

The computer was instrumental in the design process of my quilt: finding the basic idea, creating the Basket pattern, and sizing the baskets. I used the Adobe Photo Essentials program.

The photo of the fractal was the center of the quilt plan. I added the borders and made notes on that page. There was no doubt about how I was going to make the design and what would be left out. Much of my quilting is improvisational, trying new methods and revising my ideas at times. I began working on FIBONACCI NEBULA at my guild's spring retreat.

UNDERWATER BASKET WEAVING, ©2005 KEITH MACKAY

I used a yard of Ricky Tims' hand-dyed fabric in the center. I chose a point for the center of the spirals and drew them freehand. The yellow-green central short spirals were raw-edge fused and satin stitched. Iridescent polyester chiffon was carefully fused on, trapping metallic Angelina fibers underneath. The baskets were fused

I am the happiest when I am creating whether with paint or fibers.

on next. The smaller ½" baskets were hand cut with an X-Acto knife from fabric already fused on one side. The larger baskets were needle-turned hand appliqué.

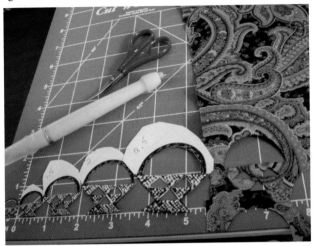

My painted fabric was fused with a paper-backed fusible webbing on the back. Spirals were drawn onto the fabric freehand and cut out so the lightest ends were at the center and the larger, darker ends would be at the outer border. These were ironed into place, and then a cording foot was used to zigzag on the raw edges with a variety of twisted metallic embroidery threads.

The first border is a narrow yellow-green commercial cotton fabric. It is an ombre fabric that moves in color from yellow to yellow-green. It is the same fabric used in the center spirals and adds a little visual movement to the quilt.

The outside border was made with a Caryl Bryer Fallert's Gradations fabric ranging from light blue to a darker blue. This fabric seemed to add a glow to the quilt. The aqua spirals were continued onto this border and grew in width.

The quilting was a challenge as the feathers branch off and change in size. I drew them out on Golden Threads Quilting Paper for each spiral section and numbered each piece so as to find its correct spot and orientation on the quilt. Picking the paper out of the tight feather corners took time and the use of a stiletto.

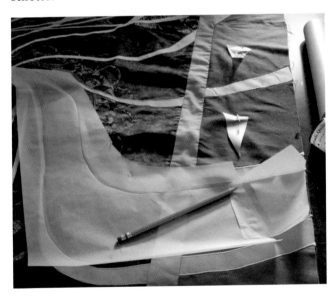

The following sums up what I have learned about art that also applies to my quilting. Nothing exists by itself. There are relationships that occur in pairs and opposites. Where there is light, there is shadow; where there is line, there is shape; where there is color, there is excitement; where there is form, there is dimension; where there is fiber, there is texture; where there is a collection of ideas, there is a collage. I am the happiest when I am creating whether with paint or fibers. I am at a stage of life where I have the luxury of making art the way I desire. The "frosting on the cake" is when someone also enjoys what I have created.

Finalist Basket Arrangements

54" x 63"

Photo by Jessica Horton

Ann Horton
Redwood Valley, California

I love baskets! I'm thinking that loving baskets must be a very close kin to loving quilts. Both are the work of caring hands, fashioned from natural materials, and provide everyday living essentials for the home. And of course, baskets and quilts also express art and beauty for the maker and the observer. How can we not love baskets?

During my early years on our farm in Illinois, baskets were everyday fare. My grandfather and my dad both used the old farm bushel baskets for everyday tasks and these baskets remain with us today. My husband uses the baskets for his garden clippings, and I use every kind of basket for holding my goods: fabric in my studio, fruit and vegetables in my kitchen, even my lunch taken to work.

Baskets also have a habit of collecting in my home. African, South American, and Native American baskets each have a personality. Living in northern California's rural Mendocino County we are blessed with a rich history of native Pomo basket making. For many indigenous cultures the world over, baskets represent essential tools of daily living, and art historians and art lovers have collected these objects of beauty throughout time. Since I also collect fabrics and love ethnic textiles, my love of both baskets and quilts happily combine in BASKET ARRANGEMENTS.

My own quiltmaking history reaches across 30 years. Even before that, I helped my grandmother tie quilts that she pieced for family and for mission donations. Ten years ago I made a large scrap basket quilt that remains one of my favorites. I love traditional quilts and contemporary art quilts and have made many of both styles. I exhibit my work in many national and international shows and have been gratified by what I have learned and shared in the process. BASKET ARRANGEMENTS is the seventh quilt I have had accepted into a New Quilts from an Old Favorite exhibit.

Inspiration

This year, I decided to tackle the challenge of making a pictorial quilt for the contest. As I thought through the history and use of baskets, I knew I wanted to depict a special scene of a family working with their baskets. I returned again to my love of Guatemalan textiles and naturally choose this beautiful cultural setting for my quilt. Guatemalan people use baskets in every facet of their daily life, and the early morning preparations for the flower market are no exception. Here we see a grandmother teaching her granddaughter how to arrange the beautiful blooms for each basket. And baskets are indeed blooming!

The quilt has 10 different baskets pieced, appliquéd, and embroidered. All the baskets reflect the textiles and style of the Guatemalan culture. The women wear their traditional clothing and are in postures that reflect their work and their relationship to one another. In this manner, the quilt tells the story of women's work, family ties, and culturally significant elements of daily life. Stone walls, steps adorned with baskets, chickens strutting through the mix, and the almost hidden lives of salamanders, birds, and bees are all present on a warm and sunny morning as the women prepare their trade.

Working with the textiles and piecing the baskets, I felt a part of their life in an intimate way. Braiding hair, an arm lifted to balance a basket, a downward look at the one empty basket waiting to be filled—all speak of a moment captured.

Technique: Filling the Baskets with Embroidery

Another confession: I love my embroidery machine! I have been utilizing machine embroidery in my quilts since 2001. What a learning process this has been! My early machine (an old Husqvarna) enticed me with its simple yet amazing set of small hoops and designs. I have progressed through two more machines and presently work on a Husqvarna Designer SE along with the software to make my designs.

Nowadays I mix purchased designs with manipulated and unique combinations, cutting and pasting and morphing my way through the design process. I also am able to digitize designs and quilting patterns and find my machine has an endless source of functions that requires constant learning curves. I have, through trial and error, practiced multitudes of ways to apply embroidery to my quilts. Each quilt design suggests and often demands a new approach to the process.

In BASKET ARRANGEMENTS, the majority of designs were embroidered separately on water-soluble stabilizer and then manipulated back onto the surface of the quilt. This is an arduous and time-consuming process that reaps certain rewards not achievable with other approaches.

First and foremost, it lets me experiment with designs before I commit them to my quilt. Secondly, it allows me to manipulate the design's placement after the embroidery is complete. This is especially important for flowers and vines that were placed in the baskets. Embroidering "off" the quilt allowed me to interweave the flowers through handles, under edges of baskets, and flow down the sides. This process also allowed me to overlap designs to create even more texture and relief on the quilt surface. I am a big fan of texture and the sculpted effect of thread on a quilt. Texture certainly comes from the quilting stitches themselves. Appliqué also provides texture and relief.

The use of the thick ethnic fabrics especially adapts to appliqué and creates a place of shadow stitching with dark, heavy cotton threads. When I fashioned the clothing, I embroidered small motifs directly to the fabric, then cut and arranged the clothing to dress the figure.

It is such a blessing to work with textiles and creative ideas, and to have the technology available to achieve the desired results.

BASKET ARRANGEMENTS was built from the ground floor up: first the background was layered and quilted, then the women were created and stitched into place, after which the baskets were settled into the scene. The embroidery was created to fill the baskets. I estimate that the embroidery alone took two months to complete. Each area of the quilt was auditioned with designs that might be appropriate. When a design was selected, careful measurements were taken to determine the size of the designs. Some embroideries, like the veining flowers in the large basket on the left, were created in multiple pieces as I kept adding segments until I had filled the area with a lush flow of vines spilling down the sides of the container.

As an example of how the embroideries were created, I will focus here on a leaf design that was added to the old-fashioned pieced basket in the lower right corner. After designing the size and style of the leaf in my software, I placed two layers of Floriani Wet N Gone water-soluble stabilizer in my hoop and transferred my design from my software to my machine to embroider.

When completed, the design was trimmed of stabilizer, soaked in warm water to remove the remaining

bits of Floriani to soften the design, and then carefully placed onto the basket for stitching.

The entire quilt was a delight to make. I felt a close kinship to the women in the quilt by the time I was done. The hours spent with them were hours I enjoyed. I felt I understood the importance of their work and the significance of the baskets in our shared daily rituals. We had many conversations about life as I fashioned their faces and hands holding the flowers.

It is such a blessing to work with textiles and creative ideas, and to have the technology available to achieve the desired results. This is a relationship I will continue to explore as long as the creative juices flow, and I have no doubt the journey will lead me to many unique stories just waiting to be told.

See more of my work at my website: annhortonquilts.com.

Finalist

Basketek
64½" x 66"

Photo by Nancy Lambert

Nancy Lambert
Pittsburgh, Pennsylvania

I have been quilting for over 25 years and enjoy all parts of the process. I find that I can sketch out far more designs than I will ever have time to complete.

I am inspired by both geometric designs and nature. Of course, nature has much repetition and geometric design inherent within a flower or bird. For many of the quilt blocks, I look at the individual pieces and what the possibilities are for repeating or scaling the individual shapes and patches to create a new design that is visually interesting.

Through quilting I have met so many wonderful people that have become such good friends and part of my life. It is hard to imagine another activity that brings together such a wonderful group of individuals.

Inspiration and Design

I was inspired to make this quilt because of the geometric nature of the basket design. The basic triangular shape that is repeated brought to mind using various sizes of triangles throughout the design. I used four different sizes of the basket design and then included multiple other sizes of an individual triangular shape. I played with adding these extra triangular shapes and placed them upside down, as compared to the large basket, to provide balance and interest. The triangular shapes were dominant at the center of the quilt, in both top corners, and at the bottom. My goal was to repeat the triangular shapes in various sizes throughout the quilt.

Additional circular shapes were added to balance the triangular shapes. Half-circles were added along both sides to complement the triangular shapes. Spiral shapes were included at the top and bottom to provide contrast and softness. Many of the fabrics used have circular shapes as part of their design.

Because this is an original design, I drew the pattern full-scale on graph paper, then created individual templates. The angles for the large triangular shapes were challenging because I was using a striped fabric and needed to match up the stripes with the unique angular pieces.

The quilting includes both outline quilting on many of the baskets and also many geometric shapes. I used circular shapes and both square and triangular grids to complement the geometric shapes within the blocks.

Technique

Mitered corner thread appliqué is a technique that I used throughout the quilt. This appliqué technique highlights a shape with colored thread satin stitch. The emphasis is on the colored thread to provide visual interest. I have two examples of how this technique is used. These include a triangular shape and a square or rectangular shape.

Square or Rectangular Shape

To machine appliqué a square shape, you usually start at one corner and follow the outline of the square. When you came to a corner you would pivot at the corner and continue on around the rest of the shape. In a mitered corner, the thread creates a miter rather than the stitching on one side being overlapped by the stitching along the next. I like the resulting clean and precise look.

The new technique creates smaller individual shapes that are stitched at a constant angle from the beginning to end. At the corners of each of these shapes you can see that the thread creates the miter.

Determine how wide you want your appliqué stitch to be. Draw a smaller square inside the original square, defining a space equal to the desired width of your satin stitch. Draw a line from the corner of the smaller square to the corner of the larger square to define the miter.

Satin stitch each side of the square, starting with a narrow width stitch at one corner, widening the stitch as you go, then decreasing the width at the opposite end of the side to create the miter. Repeat on the next 3 sides. The satin stitch is always perpendicular to the edge of the shape.

Triangular Shape

For the triangular shape the procedure is similar. From your original triangular shape, create a smaller shape by as much as you want the width of the satin stitch to be. Then connect the corners. This gives you the shapes that you can then satin stitch.

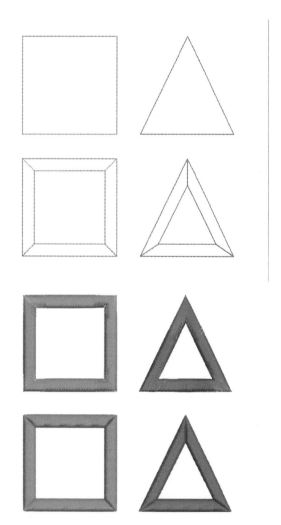

It is hard to imagine another activity that brings
together such a wonderful group of individuals.

Finalist

Sewing Baskets Inside Out

60½" x 60½"

Photo by Doug Bailey

Kathy Parker
Hudson, Florida

When it comes to quilting, my sister asked, "Where are you getting it from?" That was a good question given that none of my past or present relatives has been a sewer, artist, or quilter. I remember that my mother gave me embroidery patterns, and I wanted as many colors of embroidery floss as I could get. I also remember the Singer sewing machine salesman coming to the house to demonstrate the wonders of the latest model. My mother purchased the machine, but then did not use it, probably because she had five children and a full-time job.

At ten years old, I decided to sew my own clothes. I moved the sewing machine into my closet, found an old pink sheet, and bought a pattern for shorts and a matching top. I ran up and down stairs for about a week getting Mother to clarify sewing directions and give approval for each completed step as I assembled the parts. Believe it or not, I actually wore that outfit.

Lots of things have changed. I now make quilts instead of clothes. I use three sewing machines and have a large sewing table that goes across the entire wall of a bedroom devoted to quilting. The built-in shelves of the walk-in closet are loaded with beautiful quilt fabric and sewing notions. Since I know how to sew and prefer one-of-a-kind quilts, I no longer use purchased patterns. With me, quilting is all about the challenges of problem solving and making choices, which is what I like.

Some things never change. I still like the idea of using "old" fabric, but not sheets. Last year I found a garage sale where the quilter was selling her dated stash. I discovered a collection of solids, vintage 30s sateen, and several fabrics with symmetrical designs first seen in kaleidoscope quilts in the 1990s. Without exception, I have never had such a great time with five dollars!

I learn best by experimentation, studying quilts, and reading everything. I have never taken art or design courses, but designing quilts has become an end in itself. Every year I create a design for this competition, but have sewn only the two that were personally meaningful. I still like to use many colors together and I still make many mistakes. I consider myself an amateur quilter, a status that I enjoy.

Regarding my professional life, I am a retired speech-language pathologist. I diagnosed early childhood speech and language problems for the Albuquerque Public Schools. In my personal life, I have two grown children and two grandsons. My husband, Doug, is the love of my life. Several years ago, he took us on a spontaneous vacation that happened to wind up at The National Quilt Museum. He has read numerous books sitting outside quilt shops, and then, last summer he did the cooking to give me more time to finish the quilt for this competition. I have got it good, and I appreciate it.

Inspiration and Design

In late December of 2010, I visited the museum's website to see about the current competition results and the upcoming themes. The same day, I had been studying quilt designs and noticed some sewing objects used as motifs: spools on either side of closed scissors quilted into a border. By the next morning, I had combined "sewing" with "baskets." The challenge began.

I researched examples of Basket blocks, and later focused on shapes of baskets: triangles and circles. I thought about organizing the space on the quilt by using the contents of a sewing basket, sort of inside out. I realized open scissors provided the triangles needed to combine four baskets into a medallion setting. The concept was so playful that it was irresistible—new baskets made from old favorites, i.e., scissors, rulers, pindot fabric, and other notions.

For the top basket, a block was created from rulers to suggest overlapping baskets with a smaller one between them. On the bottom, one basket faces down and has a pointed handle, and one faces up and has a handle which is the white round band that encloses all the baskets. A third basket is outlined by the white triangles and has the curved orange thread as its handle. The small, stacked baskets within the two side dark handles were designed from mirror-image fabric prints, using Paula Nadelstern's methods in her book *Kaleidoscopes and Quilts*.

Next I needed a border. The basic component of the Goose Tracks block looked like a basket. Its diagonal piece would echo the pinking shears, and I could make large "stitches" out of the negative space created when two patches were joined.

The basic design was finished. I made the remaining choices about details as I constructed the quilt. The blue background fabric was reminiscent of pindot fabric. The zigzag quilting pattern and metallic rick-rack echo the basket triangles. The eyelet trim made of folded bias and the spools emphasize the basket handles. The little dots of the selvage edges and the gradient fabrics repeat the changing hues of the color wheel and add movement to the design.

Techniques

The most problematic aspect of this design was its construction. I had no idea how to sequence the assembly of the medallion with those shears sticking out at the corners. I also knew from experience that triangular and round shapes had stretchy bias edges that had to be controlled. Careful preparation and good sewing strategies were important to make the pieces fit.

First, I drafted the medallion and border designs onto graph paper, made a copy, and planned the best way to piece the parts of the quilt.

I cut the copy apart and glued it over a paper background and lettered each section to determine the assembly sequence. The color wheel would be appliquéd to the center after assembly of the medallion,

I learn best by experimentation, studying quilts, and reading everything.

then the medallion appliquéd to the background, and finally the border.

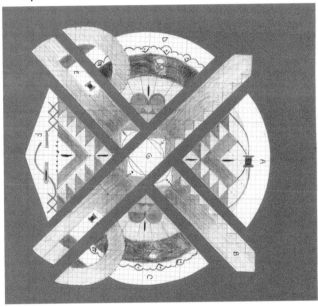

The next step in the preparation process was to develop a full size freezer-paper pattern. I ironed the freezer-paper patterns to the fabric, then marked the seam allowances and cut. When I cut the pieces for the shears from the gradient fabric, I organized the patterns so that the darker values would be at the center.

Whenever possible, I left the freezer paper on the long pieces as I sewed them together. It controlled the stretching on bias edges and guaranteed a perfect fit between adjoining parts. It also functioned as a guide when folding over the seam allowance on the long curved edges of the dark and light basket handle bands.

Rather than piecing everything, I chose to machine appliqué many of the patches. It controls stretching and the fabric can be adjusted for an exact fit, and can be more easily corrected than traditional piecing meth-

ods. For example, the lavender and blue triangles that comprise the top and bottom baskets of the medallion were sewn after the medallion was constructed so the points would exactly match the points of the serrated blades of the pinking shears, which were also appliquéd to avoid bulky seams. Appliquéing the medallion to the background was easier than cutting up the background and adjusting curves at the seam line.

Photo by Douglas L. Parker

The machine-appliqué technique is simple. Apply fusible-web strips cut less than ¼" wide under folded seam allowances following the manufacturer's instructions. Sew the patch in place using a short narrow blanket stitch. This technique adds dimension to the piecing, has a smooth finish, and can be decorative depending on the type of thread used.

Finalist

Basket Weaving
64" x 54"

Mary Kay Price
Lake Oswego, Oregon

In my 25 years as a food manufacturer, quiltmaking had never crossed my mind. After my husband's career moved us from our home in Oregon to Pennsylvania, I was on a mission to buy vacuum cleaner bags so that I could clean up our half unpacked new home. And then I saw it—LOG CABIN QUILT IN A DAY!—No Experience Necessary!—Beginners Welcome!

Photo by Larry Filz Photographer

This was just the excuse I needed to abandon my overwhelming unpacking job. My sewing machine had already made it out of its moving box. What else did I need? (*Now* I know that is a dumb question, but at the time it seemed to make sense.)

Suffice it to say, even though my Log Cabin was not built in a day, it was great fun seeing that quilt grow. To my great surprise, my first sample of quilting was much more to me than a diversion from unpacking.

Quiltmaking and quilting classes quickly became my bag of potato chips—I couldn't stop at one. I fell in with a tremendous gang of quiltmakers who shared their knowledge, friendship, and lunch with me. When it occurred to me that I felt confined by standard blocks and patterns, they shoved me out of the nest and encouraged me to develop the designs that were crowding my brain.

This is the challenge and satisfaction for me—designing and executing my own designs.

Eleven years and two more moves have passed since then. My quilting studio has gotten smaller with each move and more packed with materials and tools of the trade that I can't seem to live without. We have now returned to Oregon, via a four year stay in Chicago and another incredible quilting friend and the quilting genius of the women of PAQA (Professional Art Quilt Alliance). The journey has been grand so far but I know it is just beginning.

Now that we're with our family my quilting days are fewer, but I get into my studio three or four days a week. My children and grandchildren see my work with new eyes and are happy to share their unvarnished opinions with me.

Contests and judge's comment sheets are another good source of information to improve my work. It was from judging comments that I learned bindings should feel full and that the mitered corners should be stitched tight by hand. Another thing that I learned from the judges is that I occasionally disagree with them, and that's healthy too.

Over the last couple years I have done more realistic work. I do that in parallel with my abstract designs. Not sure where this double track is going. Perhaps they will collide. We will see.

For most of my work, I prefer to keep raising the bar for myself on the quality of craftsmanship and execution. It is distracting to see a stunning design constructed poorly.

It is a good exercise to do a quilting challenge, such as New Quilts From an Old Favorite. Using someone else's parameters gets the brain thinking in another direction.

I will never forget my Log Cabin quilt class in Pennsylvania. It opened a whole universe of beauty and artistry for me. While I don't take quilt block classes anymore, I do treat myself to a week-long seminar with one instructor every year. Spending a whole week with one instructor is a great little education. I return from these trips with new information, full of ideas, refreshed, and ready to work with abandon.

Inspiration, Design, and Technique

When I learned this year's block was Baskets, the first thought that went through my mind was my father calling any college class he considered too easy "Basket Weaving 101." But whenever he said that, I couldn't suppress the notion that it would be fascinating and possibly complex to study basket weaving.

It was with this thought that I began designing BASKET WEAVING. Each Basket block is either woven or has the textural nature of having been woven. Each Basket block is unique in style, size, color, and appearance.

Baskets are meant to carry or contain. Since I wanted to incorporate the pure hue red, these baskets carry tomatoes (or, if you are my granddaughter, red rubber balls).

The original sketch for this quilt is more loose and rough edged. I might yet make a quilt true to this sketch. However, for this challenge I opted to make each basket in more of a crisp block and sash each with striped fabric.

Photo by Larry Filz

Next was my opportunity to try my hand at two-dimensional basket weaving. How do I get the fabric to emphasize the very textural nature of handmade baskets? One technique was to lay down strips of fabric, ribbons, and yarns and weave them together. I stabilized the woven bits by fusing them to interfacing. Once fused, I could treat my woven bits as a solid piece of fabric.

Fabric choices need to support a woven appearance as well. Kaffe Fassett's shot cottons are woven with one color thread in the warp and another color in the weft. The result is a solid color but with more texture and it catches the light a little differently from varying angles. This effect is present in his solids, stripes, and plaids. Limiting myself to these fabrics and a couple of hand-dyed sets provided a subtle color palette. Except for my red tomatoes, there are no pure hues.

The remainder of the baskets are constructed with stripes and plaids—some cut in strips, some on the bias, some short, some tall, some wide, some squat, some with handles and some without. There is no need to have any repeated basket.

Beginning the construction of my Basket blocks I found my fabrics were too soft. My blocks were going to be limp and would not have the structural, substantial look I was after. To resolve this challenge I borrowed a page from Jane Sassaman and fused all the fabrics to Pellon Shir-Tailor fusible interfacing. Now each block was substantial. There would be no twisting or bunching while I used 30-wt. cotton threads to encase all the raw edges in a satin stitch.

My preference is to machine quilt densely, with great detail. It seemed to me that dense quilting would distract from the baskets. Instead, I stitched with 12-wt. cotton threads on the sides of each satin stitch. Over that I added widely spaced wavy lines of thread. Those two supported the look of the simple structure I was after.

This is the challenge and satisfaction for me –
designing and executing my own designs.

Finalist

Spinning Baskets
64" x 54"

Theresea Reeves
Oberlin, Kansas

Photo by James L. Reeves

I was raised on a farm in northwest Kansas and have spent my entire life in this area. Growing up I was interested in sewing as it was a part of our farm life and I enjoyed watching my mother sew. My first attempt at sewing was to make garments while I was in high school. I carried this acquired skill into my adult life by making clothes for my family.

I started quilting 20 years ago after a stressful time in my life left me with free time to fill. I love the traditional patterns, color, fabric, and texture and the joy it brings to sew them into something beautiful. After making many quilts from a pattern I was ready to try designing one of my own. That attempt was a success in that I placed second in Keepsake Quilting's Christmas theme contest in 1997. I was a finalist in the Sunflower: New Quilts from an Old Favorite contest in 2009 and have won or placed in many regional quilt contests over the years.

Since I entered my first contest I have designed many of my own quilts and will continue to do so as I love the challenge. This contest is perfect—you have a quilt block to design from, there are no rules, you do as your heart desires with the only pressure being the deadline. I will have to say that quilting is very much a part of my life. I have operated a successful longarm quilting business for the last nine years and I plan to continue in my business and the design of my own quilts for many more years. I have also conducted numerous quilt classes and trunk shows throughout northwest Kansas and southwest Nebraska over the last 15 years.

Being a collector of Longaberger baskets I was inspired by this year's contest. After looking at the various baskets in my collection, I settled on the working style basket presented here. I love working with small pieces and making miniature quilts, so it seemed only natural to use a miniature block in my design. I have taken two years of art classes at McCook Community College and from that I have learned how to work with color. The black background in my quilt works well with the warm colors—red and yellow—that I used for the baskets to cause them to stand out from the shades of blue that were used for the pinwheels throughout the quilt. The small amounts of red fabric through the quilt stand out to stop the spinning motion of the pinwheels and redirect your attention to the baskets.

The basic element in the traditional Basket block is the half-square triangle. With this in mind I rearranged the half-square triangles to form a Pinwheel block. I used Thangles to piece the 1" and 2" Pinwheel blocks and also the ½" Sawtooth interior borders. I continued to add pinwheels in the background to give a sense of motion and used them as flowers in the basket. I hand embroidered greenery and the hummingbirds feeding on the nectar. The vines flow from the basket into the background, helping to draw your attention outside the basket. The handle of the basket was made by trial and error. I used a red and yellow bias strip twisted to form

Since I entered my first contest, I have designed many of my own quilts and will continue to do so as I love the challenge.

a handle that I hand appliquéd to the basket. The black background makes all the other colors pop.

After designing and sewing the first block, the rest of the quilt was designed as I sewed it together. One thing much different about this quilt is the setting. Unlike most quilt blocks that are set corner to corner, mine are set half-side to half-side. (See the pattern photo.)

Since I have an unusual setting, I need to fill in the half-block space. This is done throughout the quilt with 1" finished strips connecting the 1" pinwheels and the 1" pinwheels overlapping into the 2" pinwheels. The 2" pinwheels are made to spin in the opposite direction, adding a sense of motion to the quilt.

The red diagonal strips were added to control the spinning motion and redirect your focus to the hummingbirds feeding on the flowers in the baskets. The scalloped edge was used to help soften the motion as your eye leaves the quilt.

When it came time to machine quilt, I continued the hummingbird theme to the corners by sketching them into a feather pattern. I enhanced them with trapunto to add a sense of dimension to the quilting. A black metallic thread was used throughout to add a little sparkle. I sewed small glass beads in the center of the blue pinwheels and the flowers in the baskets. I also applied crystals in the vine and various parts of the quilt to give it glimmer and shine.

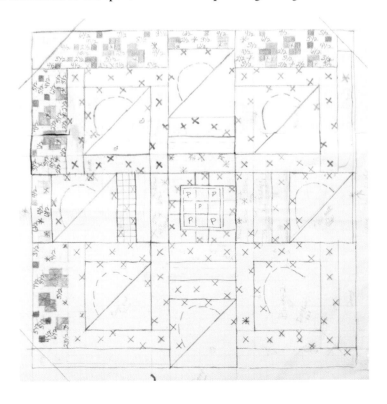

Finalist

Baskets, Butterflies, and Blossoms

71" x 73"

Tish Rudd
Cadiz, Kentucky

The seeds of my quilting life were planted years ago by my mother and grandmothers. I remember as a young child being so proud of the special Easter dresses that my mother made for my sister and me. Mom was also an avid knitter, making everything from socks for my father to sweaters to match our wool skirts. Later in life she began quilting, preferring stamped cross-stitch and appliqué patterns, and hand quilting.

Photo by Bruce Rudd

I remember watching my maternal grandmother cut and hand appliqué her quilts. I was amazed at how she made her stitches "disappear" into the fabric. She loved to appliqué, but "sent her quilts out" to be hand quilted by a friend. My paternal grandmother was an accomplished seamstress. She made her own wedding dress at the turn of the 20th century, most of the clothing for her 13 children, and designed and hooked her own rugs. We still have a quilt that she made using scraps from her daughters' dresses.

My first experiences with sewing began with doing hand embroidery in Girl Scouts and making an apron in 4-H. My mother said that she didn't think I would ever finish either project because I became bored quickly with repetitive activities and wanted to hurry up and get finished so I could try something else.

Upon retiring and moving full-time to our vacation home on Lake Barkley in western Kentucky, I began searching for a new creative outlet and a way to make friends in our new location. That's when a friend invited me to my first quilt guild meeting. The seed that had been planted years ago by those wonderful women in my life blossomed into what has become my passion—quilting! Mom was really shocked when I began making quilts, but I have learned to enjoy the process of creating a quilt as much as the finished project.

I became interested in trying to design my own quilts. I attended a Ricky Tims lecture at the 2011 AQS Quilt Show in Paducah. He explained the design technique he used to create his Rhapsody quilts.

Now here was something that excited me. That afternoon while I was volunteering at The National Quilt Museum, I saw the brochure for the contest. It didn't take long for me to realize that I could put a new design technique and my love for appliqué together and start a whole new adventure in quilting. Six months later BASKETS, BUTTERFLIES, AND BLOSSOMS was finished. I am excited to see where my quilting adventure takes me next.

Inspiration and Design

I have always been interested in Baltimore Album quilts. Some of my favorite quilts at The National Quilt Museum in Paducah are the album quilts. After making one of these Baltimore beauties by hand, I realized that the traditional method was not for me. That is when I began exploring construction options. Fused, raw-edge appliqué was the answer. I found this method gave me the end look that I was wanting and the process itself is very satisfying.

The Ricky Tims method (see his book, *Rhapsody Quilts*) gave me the design tool to take BASKETS in a whole new direction. I knew it would give me the symmetry and movement that I was looking for. My next inspiration was to use fabrics that were bold and vibrant. The cotton hand-dyed fabrics from the Ricky Tims collection provided intense saturated colors for the background pieces. Commercial batiks used in the appliqué gave me the contrast I was looking for.

Finally, I decided to use contrasting rayon machine embroidery thread for the topstitching to make the appliqué shapes pop. Decorative stitches on some of the appliqués would give them additional depth.

I have no pre-construction pictures or design drawings for this project because I literally designed it as I went.

I planned to free-motion quilt my project using my HQ Sixteen and cotton thread that would blend with the background fabrics. I wanted the quilting to create more texture in the background than color. I decided to use black cotton batting.

Technique

I find fused raw-edged appliqué a quite enjoyable process. The first step in this process is to prepare the appliqué pieces. I prewash all fabrics that I plan on using for fused appliqué and I do not use fabric softener in the rinse. The fusible web adheres much better when sizing has been removed from the fabric.

I prefer lightweight Wonder Under for fusing. For small pieces, I let the fusible cover the whole back of the appliqué. However, for large pieces, I "window" the fusible to reduce stiffness in the appliqué.

Trace the appliqué pattern onto the paper side of a fusible web.

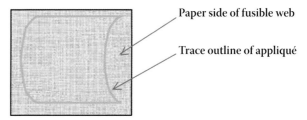

Paper side of fusible web

Trace outline of appliqué

Draw an interior cutting line on the INSIDE of the traced line and cut away excess fusible web.

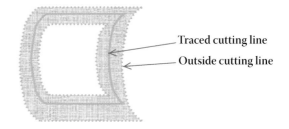

Interior cutting line

Cut out the traced pattern leaving a scant ¼" border on the outside.

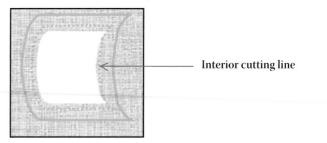

Traced cutting line

Outside cutting line

Press the pattern onto the wrong side of the fabric. Now cut out the piece on the traced line.

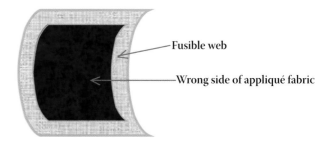

Fusible web

Wrong side of appliqué fabric

The appliqué piece is ready to fuse to the background fabric.

Begin topstitching around the outside of the appliqué. I use a clear open-toe embroidery foot and a size 12 needle in my machine. For this project I used con-

I have learned to enjoy the process of creating a quilt as much as the finished project.

trasting embroidery thread in both the top and bobbin. The needle-down setting on your machine is a must. A knee lift also saves much time. Always start stitching away from the corner of your appliqué piece.

I like using the blanket stitch on my Brother Innovis 2800D Sewing Machine. I can regulate both the width and length of the stitch. Practice with your machine until you are comfortable with the pattern of your stitching. For the blanket stitch, my machine stitches forward, back, forward, left, right. This will be very important when you are stitching corners. Keep your vertical stitches as close as possible to the right edge of your appliqué without piercing the appliqué. The horizontal stitches should be perpendicular to the edge stitches, especially along curves. On curves, after sewing the straight stitches, with the needle down lift the presser foot and pivot slightly so the next stitch will be toward the center of the curve.

Once I get into a rhythm, I actually find this very relaxing.

Finalist

Handle With Care

58" x 59"

Photo by Gary Soules

Jan Soules
Elk Grove, California

I knew how to sew long before I became a quilter. As a child, I remember playing on the lawn making doll clothes because we couldn't afford to buy them. I picked up sewing skills from a friend's mom. I received a new Singer sewing machine as a high school graduation present. It was to die for! I still have it!

As I grew up, I gradually stopped sewing and found other hobbies, and travel and living abroad occupied my time. My true quilting career began in 2000, when my expectant daughter asked me to make a baby quilt for my first granddaughter, Isabelle. Little did I know what that quilt would lead to.

I became passionate immediately and started taking every class I could. Each year I go to the Empty Spools quilt seminar in Pacific Grove, California. I've been able to spend time with wonderful teachers and particularly credit my classes with Judy Mathieson, Ruth McDowell, and Diane Gaudynski as having an influence on my work—Judy for her precise piecing and attention to detail, Ruth for her sense of fabric blending, and Diane for giving me the confidence to quilt my own quilts. They are each legends in their own fields and I feel lucky that I got a chance to study with each of them in a beautiful, relaxed setting.

People often ask me how I get so much done. It's an easy question to answer. I set aside time for quilting every day. I like to be in my studio from 1:00 to 5:00 each afternoon. I watch TV while I sew. At the beginning of each month, I set monthly goals and post them near my calendar. Then each day, I set smaller daily goals. I divide my time into one hour segments between several projects. This keeps me on target and doesn't let me become bored on any one type of task. I piece and design during the afternoon and work on hand appliquéing projects in the evening in front of the TV. This combination seems to work for me. It's amazing how much you can get done.

In addition to my love of quilting, I am an expert tournament bridge player and travel around the country with my husband, Gary, for competitions. I also enjoy reading and exercising and am currently trying to teach my two granddaughters, Isabelle and Sophie, how to sew. They are naturals!

Inspiration and Design

How excited I was to find out the contest theme for 2012 was baskets. It was tailor-made for me. My granddaughter Isabelle, age 11, worked on a large quilt with me called BASKETS 101. She helped remove the paper pieces when the top was done and has since laid claim to that bright and cheerful quilt.

Granddaughter Isabelle with BASKETS 101, photographed with permission of her mom

That quilt was my starting inspiration. My original rough sketch for HANDLE WITH CARE shows a large center basket surrounded by baskets that turn around the quilt. In the final version, I grouped the baskets two by two, and marched them around the center basket. This gave the quilt movement and direction in a circular motion. My intention was to design a fun, quirky quilt, and I tried to keep that in mind during each stage of the design process.

Did the colors of my quilt grab your attention? I hope so. I again wanted to have fun. I had a large stash of red fabrics, so it was natural to turn to that as a background color. I contrasted it with a mix of bright turquoises to create a visual pop! I loved the combination and felt it suited these off-beat baskets with the broken handles.

One design decision that gave me some problems toward the end was what, if anything, I should put in the baskets. I ended up simply quilting flowers into the baskets and sprinkling the flower shapes in and out of the border on two sides.

Broken Basket Block

The main body of HANDLE WITH CARE is composed of 16 baskets that twist and turn around a slightly larger center basket. The blocks are made in sets of two in a freeform manner so that no two are identical. I refer to the process as Make It, Break It, and Remake It, and it can be adapted to any size. The extra block from the larger center block was placed on the back of the quilt as "back art."

Make It:

Step 1: Body of the basket (Piece 1)
Cut several strips of blue fabrics. Vary length and width.
Cut a triangle shape for the center, about 1½"–2" per side.

Sew a strip of blue fabric to one side of the triangle. Press away from the triangle and trim on the diagonal. Turn the block and repeat. Repeat this process until you have the approximate size you want.

Step 2: Adding background and basket base
Place a piece of red background fabric on your cutting mat.
Place the blue triangle from step 1 on top, making sure to leave fabric on all sides.
Using the triangle as a guide, place your ruler along the side edges and cut the red fabric along the edges, one side at a time. You will have 3 pieces: a left background, the triangle, and a right background piece.
Cut a triangle off the bottom of each background piece, on a slant going away from the basket.

Use the triangles as a template to cut bases from a blue fabric. Sew them to the background triangles. Sew the pieced background triangles to the basket triangle using a ¼" seam allowance. The wedges will overlap at the bottom where they meet. **Do Not Trim!**

Step 3: Basket handles (Piece 2)
Apply fusible web of your choice to blue handle fabrics.
Draw handle shapes on the fusible side and then cut out on the lines.
Place the handle on a piece of red background fabric approximately the same size as piece 1. Fuse, then machine buttonhole stitch the handle in place.

Step 4: Complete basket
Join the basket and handle units.
Do not trim or square up!

My intention was to design a fun, quirky quilt, and I tried to keep that in mind during each stage of the design process.

Break It

Take 2 completed Baskets blocks and stack them together right-sides up—*not* right sides together!

Starting at the bottom of the stacked pieces, cut away from yourself through the center of the blocks in a gentle curve. You may use a freezer-paper template as a guide if free form cutting scares you. You will now have 4 pieces.

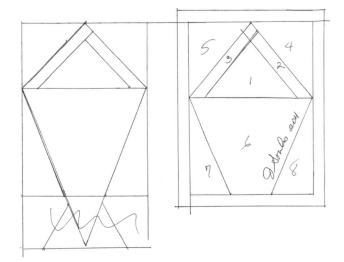

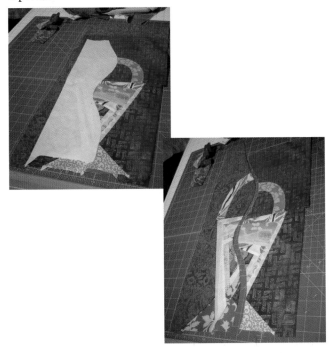

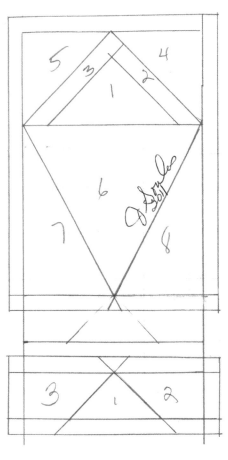

Re-make it

Take half of one block and sew it to half of the second block. Repeat. Press flat. Square and trim to size.

You now have a completed Broken Basket block. Hint: Do not try to match the basket parts or handles. You are creating a unique basket!

Finalist

Basket Case

50" x 50"

Photo by Ken West

Sue Turnquist
Tifton, Georgia

It's been a roller coaster ride, but I'm finally living the life that every married female quilter would trade half her stash for. It's been eight years since I abandoned quilting. Life happens, and before you know it, you are middle-aged (and not getting any younger), maybe wiser, and you start to look back and reflect on some of your life decisions.

I changed careers eight years ago thinking that I would have a better income and, by default, more time to quilt. I was so wrong!!! An aging mother and a topsy-turvy job with a big drug company threw a few monkey wrenches into my plans (not the quilt block kind, either!). My mom was my biggest quilting supporter, and, when she passed away in 2009, I started dwelling on everything in my life that hadn't gone just exactly as I had hoped. I blamed everybody but myself.

As I was emerging from this dark period, I was offered a leadership position with the company. My first inclination was to run for the hills, but I took the job and realized there was a whole 'nother person living in this body that I knew nothing about. I was actually a competent manager, and I was fortunate to have a boss who recognized my potential and supported me wholeheartedly.

Other life-changing events occurred, and I finally realized that having a high-paying career isn't necessarily the key to happiness. I missed being a professor and diagnostic veterinary pathologist and began applying for jobs at universities and veterinary labs across the United States. I hit the proverbial jackpot and several institutions were interested in my services—at half my industry salary and roughly half the benefits. The salary was still more than I expected, and I was elated.

I joined the University of Georgia Tifton Veterinary Diagnostic Laboratory and moved to southern Georgia, and I'm having the time of my life. My walls are covered in quilts, and most of the first floor of my house is devoted to my quilting studio. After 30 years of perpetual togetherness, my husband and I are residing in separate states. He's learning how to clean and cook for himself (we're trading recipes back and forth regularly), and I'm rediscovering my creative side. My Australian Shepherd, Jesse, is my constant companion—at home and work. I continue to be amazed at how things in the quilting world have changed during my eight-year absence.

Inspiration and Design

BASKET CASE is my re-entry into the world of competitive quilting—a world I have dearly missed. I was still unpacking when I saw the call for entries, about a month before the deadline. No problem. My fabric was still packed along with the equipment and supplies that I hadn't touched in years. No problem. I sketched the design, copied the drawing onto a transparency, and projected it on the wall with an overhead projector.

I spent one weekend digging through my fabric stash (not easy when it's divided up into 50 packing boxes). Fortunately, the batiks were mostly packed together. I spent another day visiting local quilt shops ("local" being a relative term as there aren't too many quilt shops in southern Georgia) to fill in the gaps. I formulated a schedule in my head that required that I piece one element every night after work. So far so good.

One entire weekend was devoted to assembling the pieced elements. Skills that I hadn't used in years were suddenly called to the forefront, and, given my recent spate of senior moments, I was amazed at how easily the skills returned and seemed to work almost flawlessly. Halloween weekend was spent quilting, binding and photographing the finished piece. The only thing missing was the stamina for marathon quilting sessions. My neck and posterior regions complained bitterly after a day or two of all-day quilting sessions.

Technique

I traced my design onto freezer paper, adding registration marks to facilitate reassembly. Then the freezer-paper pattern was cut up to use as templates. The templates were ironed onto the back of fabrics and/ or used as paper-piecing templates depending on each individual design element.

Many moons ago, I had a week-long class with Caryl Bryer Fallert, and I have since embraced her Appli-piecing technique. This technique involves the use of liquid starch and an iron to turn the fabric under on the paper template. A light box is used to align adjacent fabrics (using registration marks on the templates), and Scotch tape holds the aligned pieces until they can be stitched together. The fabric units are subsequently top-stitched together with invisible thread and a tiny zigzag stitch.

When I left the quilting world, I was still taking slide photos of my work and then rushing around to find a processing lab where I could get them developed immediately. I was relieved to see that quilting has reached the digital age, and that I wouldn't have to try to find a one-hour slide film developer—if those even exist.

I drew the center block sketch on the rough side of the freezer paper keeping in mind that the image would be reversed once the piece was assembled. While the sketch was drawn as shown, I made some adaptations on the fly in order to simplify the pattern for more rapid assembly.

I continue to be amazed at how things in the quilting world have changed during my eight-year absence.

Finalist

Hopi Maiden

65" x 65"

Karen Watts
Mayhill, New Mexico

Photo by Mark Ferring

I have enjoyed entering the New Quilts from an Old Favorite contest for several years now. I love the way it inspires me to reach for something different. I'm in my 20th year of quilting, and there is always something new to learn or try. This is the quilt that almost didn't happen. But, just as it takes a village to raise a child, sometimes it takes a quilting community to make a quilt.

I had been working on the design amidst the chaos of trying to upgrade our house in Houston for sale. My husband retired in March of 2011 and we decided to move permanently to our second home in the mountains of New Mexico. We had started building a free-standing quilt studio but construction had stalled and the studio was not complete. We decided to move anyway.

We did our best to downsize, we really did! But we arrived in New Mexico with *way* too much stuff. Worst of all, my fabric, sewing supplies, and the disassembled Gammill went into the garage. At least I had packed some fabric I thought I might want to use in a separate box, so I set up a little sewing area in our bedroom and got started.

What a challenge! In between unpacking boxes and trying to arrange furniture, I attempted to work on my baskets. This entailed multiple trips to the garage for different fabric, rooting through boxes for that piece I just knew was in there *somewhere!* I had no design wall (essential for designing, in my opinion), and I missed the feedback from my friends in my Bee back in Houston.

When I went to Houston in August, I got great ideas from my Bee friends, just as I knew I would. Thank you Kris, Lea Ann, Patty, and Tonda! One thing I hadn't decided how to do was the girl's face and hands. Luckily Lea Ann's daughter is a fabulous artist and colored the face and hands for me. Thank you, Sarah!

With my Gammill still in pieces, I spent a week with Kris and used her Innova longarm. The last bits of quilting were done on my trusty Pfaff 6270. I'm looking forward to the next challenge!

Inspiration and Design

I've loved the designs of Native American baskets for many years. I knew I wanted to combine the round baskets with more traditional baskets that I had redesigned to have a more southwestern "flavor." I chose a layout that allowed the round baskets to revolve around the center, with the other baskets pieced into the corners.

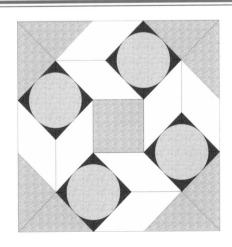

The round baskets needed 15" to incorporate the detail that the designs required, and that determined the size of the quilt. I had recently taken a workshop that used the 10-degree wedge ruler, and decided that would be my method for constructing the baskets. I printed out blank baskets and started shading with a pencil.

The diamond-shaped blocks needed to be in keeping with the southwestern look, so I drew two versions. The first proved to be very difficult to piece accurately, and I was running out of time, so I went with version 2!

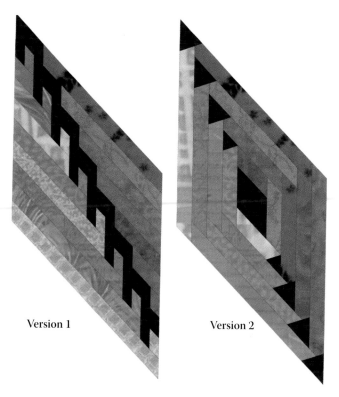

Version 1   Version 2

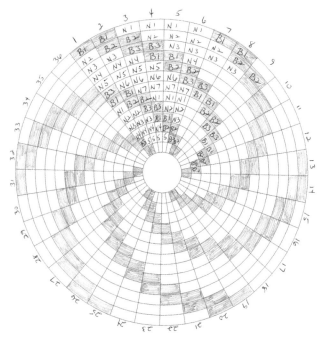

I drew the corner blocks using strips with a jagged edge, then incorporated the baskets into the strips so they could be pieced into the block, rather than laid on top.

I pieced a simple Log Cabin block for the Hopi maiden background, then put together the entire quilt top without the corners before I added the girl, as I wanted her to be larger than the center block.

From the beginning the colors were turquoise, red, and black, which are traditional colors for many tribes. But after I had the whole top pieced the border gave me trouble. As is often the case, the piece of fabric I had intended to use all along—a beautiful southwestern border stripe—did not go with the quilt after all. The quilt told me it just needed black in the border, so I listened.

Technique

The round Indian baskets are constructed of 36 wedges, 10 degrees each. Each wedge is cut from strata of 12

Just as it takes a village to raise a child, sometimes it takes a quilting community to make a quilt.

strips of fabric, each strip ½" wide finished. I chose to paper piece the strata to keep these ½" strips accurate and ensure that all the seam intersections would meet.

I analyzed each basket to determine the repeat and how many wedges I'd need to cut from each strata. I also paid attention to the starting place—top or bottom—so that the seam allowances would alternate and nest when I sewed the wedges together.

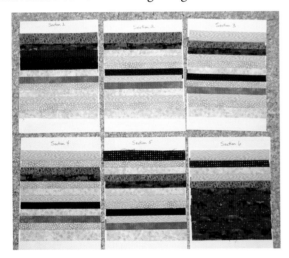

Half the strata for just one basket, shown below

The other half (not shown) are the same fabrics but with the seam allowances going in the opposite direction. Each of these strata had 3 wedges cut from them, for a total of 36 wedges.

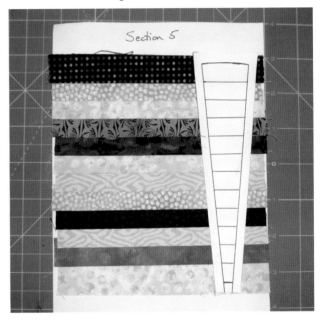

Once I had all the wedges cut from the strata, I laid them out and sewed them together in sections. These seam allowances were all pressed in the same direction, so they traveled around the circle.

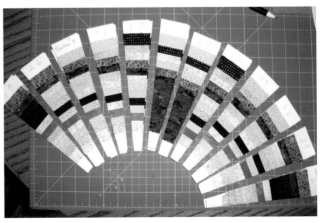

Before I applied the circle to its background, I sewed the red background pieces to two of the diamond-shaped blocks, thus avoiding a lot of set-in seams. Then I pinned the circle in place on the background and sewed a very narrow bias strip to the edge, exactly like binding a quilt. I folded the strip over, and hand sewed the other edge down. The center circles were appliquéd in place.

Resources

Check with your local quilt shop for these items.

Adobe
www.adobe.com
Adobe® Photoshop® Family of products

Amazon
www.amazon.com
Crayola® Washable Markers
Simplicity® Bias Tape Maker

Bryerpatch Studio
www.bryerpatch.com
Caryl Bryer Fallert's Gradations and
    Ombre Stripe fabrics

Dharma Trading Company
www.dharmatrading.com
Pebeo® Setacolo® paints
Dye-Na-Flow Silk Paints
PFD (prepared for dyeing) fabric

Electric Quilt 7
www.electricquilt.com
Quilt design software

Floriani Wet N Gone water-soluble stabilizer
available at your local quilt shop

Fons & Porter
www.shopfonsandporter.com
chalk markers

Golden Threads
www.goldenthreads.com
Golden Threads Quilting Paper

On One Software
www.ononesoftware.com

Photo Essentials 4: Five essential add-ons for Adobe®
Photoshop® Elements

Pellon
www.pellonideas.com
fusible, non-woven interfacing
Pellon® 950F Shir-Tailor® fusible web
Firm Fusible Interfacing
Wonder Under

Prym Consumer USA, Inc.
www.dritz.com
Dritz® Liquid Stitch™ adhesive

Renae Hadaddin
Quilts on the Corner
http://quiltsonthecorner.com
Amazing Rays tool

Ricky Tims
www.rickytims.com
Poly Stable Stuff®
Books, patterns, fabrics, and more

Sulky
www.sulky.com
Sulky® Totally Stable® Iron-On, Tear-Away Stabilizer

Superior Threads
www.superiorthreads.com
Razzle Dazzle™ thread by Ricky Tims

Thangles
www.thangles.com
Thangles foundation paper strips for half-square triangle construction

The National Quilt Museum

The National Quilt Museum is the world's largest and most prestigious museum devoted to quilts and fiber art. Established in 1991, the Museum is committed to the preservation and advancement of quilting. In an average year, the Museum is visited by quilters and art enthusiasts from all 50 states and over 40 countries around the world.

Located in a 27,000 square foot facility in historic downtown Paducah, Kentucky, the Museum's three galleries feature exhibits of the finest quilt and fiber art in the world. The Museum's vibrant and breathtaking exhibits are rotated 10–12 times per year. Our primary gallery, with over 7,000 square feet of exhibit space, features quilts from the Museum's permanent collection that includes over 320 works of art. Our two other galleries feature touring exhibits of unique and diverse quilts and fiber art.

The Museum has also gained a reputation for its educational programs. Throughout the year, the Museum hosts educational programs on a diverse number of topics for quilters at all skill levels. Quilters come from all over the world to attend the Museum's educational programs taught by master quilters.

The Museum's youth education programs are attended by over 4,000 young people of all ages. Several of these programs have received national media attention. The School Block Challenge, sponsored by Moda Fabrics, is an annual contest in

Student in workshop

is truly an exhilarating place to learn more about quilts, quiltmaking, and quilters.

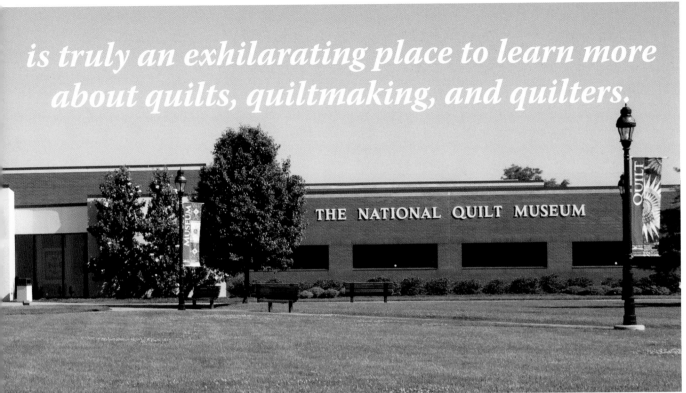

which participants are challenged to make a quilt block out of a packet of three fabrics. Now in its 17th year, this challenge continues to be utilized by schools and community organizations as part of their art curriculums in over 20 states. Other popular youth programs include the annual Quilt Camp for Kids, Kidz Day in the Arts, and the Junior Quilters and Textile Artists Club.

Gift shop manager Pamela Hill and volunteer Loyce Lovvo

Instructor Velda Newman with student

If you are reading these words, you are most likely one of over 21 million quilters in the United States and around the world. The National Quilt Museum is committed to supporting your work and expanding the vision of quilting for years to come.

For more information about
The National Quilt Museum visit our website at
www.quiltmuseum.org.

More AQS Books

This is only a small selection of the books available from the American Quilter's Society. AQS books are known worldwide for timely topics, clear writing, beautiful color photos, and accurate illustrations and patterns. The following books are available from your local bookseller, quilt shop, or public library.

#8152

#8350

#8346

#8347

#8525

#8244

#8530

#8672

#8353